The Digital Dollar Dilemma

The Digital Dollar Dilemma

CBDCs and the End of Cash

Othman Verdan

Mindful Pages

Published in 2026

ISBN: 9789374591178 (PB)
ISBN: 9789374591086 (eBook)

Published by

Mindful Pages
Imprint of Alpha Editions LLC
312 W. 2nd St #1834
Casper, WY 82601, USA

This book was developed using advanced writing tools to support the drafting and ideation process. All content has been thoughtfully curated, refined, and reviewed to ensure quality and relevance.

Content

Introduction

The first signs of a society's future are often found in the smallest exchanges. Consider a crowded street corner where a vendor hands back a few coins to a customer during a blackout. No terminals, no network, no clearance queue—just metal and trust. A few kilometres away, on that same day, thousands of workers wait anxiously because a bank's servers have stalled, freezing salary payments across the city. One system hums on despite the darkness; the other stalls, indifferent to human need. These two moments, so mundane and easily overlooked, capture a truth that policymakers and technologists sometimes forget: money is only as reliable as the infrastructure beneath it, and the infrastructure is only as just as the values that govern it.

Now imagine a future in which the simplest transactions depend not on the exchange of objects or the handshake of institutions but on lines of code written far from the lives they affect. A future in which money may settle instantly yet may also disappear at midnight by design; a future in which your wallet speaks to the state more fluently than to you; a future in which the pound in your hand is no longer a physical token but a permissioned digital signal whose conditions can change without your noticing. This is the promise—and the peril—of central bank digital currencies, or CBDCs. They sit at the convergence of finance, technology, civil liberties, and state power. They offer possibilities of remarkable public benefit: smoother payments, greater inclusion, more resilient crisis response. They also carry risks that cannot be wished away: surveillance, silent policy drift, fragility concentrated in a single point of failure, and new forms of control disguised as efficiency.

The digital pound or dollar may be coded, but it is not inevitable. It is a choice—one that demands scrutiny, imagination, and honesty. Around the world, central banks push forward with pilots and prototypes, eager to modernise ageing payment rails and catch up with the speed of private innovation. Citizens, by contrast, often hear about CBDCs only in fragments: a headline about "programmable money", a rumour about "expiry dates", a promise of "inclusion". The debate lurches between utopian optimism and dystopian fear, rarely pausing to ask the questions that matter most: What kind of money strengthens a free society? Where should programmability end and personal autonomy begin? How can we preserve the virtues of cash—its resilience, its privacy, its independence from power—while acknowledging the opportunities of the digital age?

This book sets out to bring coherence to a conversation that is too important to leave to specialists. It does not assume that a state digital currency is good or bad by default; rather, it provides the analytical tools to judge its design, its governance, and its consequences. It asks what society gains, what it risks, and what it must demand before giving consent to a system that may shape the very boundaries of economic freedom for generations. At its core lies a simple conviction: the design of money is never just about payments. It is about the architecture of trust.

To understand the stakes, it helps to recall that money was not always the invisible, frictionless construct we treat it as today. In earlier centuries, money meant a heavy purse or a scribbled IOU, and trust rested on the integrity of individuals or the authority of institutions visible in the square. As banking matured, the ledger became the decisive mechanism. What mattered was not the coin itself but the record of who held what. Over time, money dematerialised into entries, then into packets of information, then into a pulse on a server. The story of modern finance is the story of the ledger gaining prominence. Today, the ledger is not merely a record; it is the product. It determines who can transact, what is visible, what can be reversed, and what can be denied. The question posed by CBDCs is therefore not just technical but constitutional: who controls the ledger of society, and under what constraints?

The arrival of programmable value adds another layer of complexity. Once money is code, it can be conditioned. A payment can depend on behaviour, timing, location, or identity. This unlocks new forms of public administration—automatic tax rebates, targeted subsidies, faster relief during emergencies. It also raises the spectre of rules that creep without oversight. When payments can be modified remotely, how do we ensure that economic incentives are debated democratically rather than delivered silently through wallet updates? When everything is linkable, how do we guard against retrospective scrutiny of entirely lawful choices? These tensions run through the heart of the book.

Yet the conversation about CBDCs cannot be understood purely through the lens of risk. There is a real and widespread frustration with the financial plumbing we live with today. Small merchants wait days for card settlements that erode slender margins. Migrant workers lose a chunk of their income to expensive remittance providers. Citizens in remote areas struggle with outages that close local branches while promising "digital-first" services fail to deliver. Crisis payments arrive late or not at all because legacy systems cannot route funds quickly enough when it matters most. Policymakers see CBDC as an opportunity to rebuild the pipes from the ground up—a public infrastructure for money that is fast, affordable, and robust. The aspiration is not misguided. But whether the outcome is emancipatory or intrusive depends entirely on the choices made at each layer of design.

Across continents, central banks have taken diverging paths. Some favour account-based models tied closely to existing financial institutions; others explore token-based systems that mimic aspects of cash. Some emphasise privacy-preserving techniques; others prioritise traceability. These disagreements are not technical squabbles but reflections of deeper philosophies about the relationship between the state and the individual. Money has always mirrored power. The digital era simply makes the mirror clearer.

Throughout this book, one motif will serve as a guide: the wallet as constitution. For centuries, constitutional rights were enforced on paper and in courtrooms; today, the practical enforcement of economic freedom may depend just as much on the software through which we transact. A right expressed in legislation but contradicted by the wallet's defaults is not a right enjoyed in practice. If privacy is the norm in principle but optional in configuration, the pressure of convenience and design may erode it for most citizens. If autonomy is promised yet conditionality is coded, the boundary between choice and coercion blurs. The wallet is where rules meet reality, and its design determines whether a CBDC becomes a tool of empowerment or an instrument of paternalism.

This motif connects to a broader theme: resilience. Cash has an unappreciated elegance—it survives storms, outages, and political shifts. It is a decentralised, low-tech, high-trust device for continuity. A digital currency must earn its place by matching that resilience or offering compensating advantages. The more society centralises its monetary rail, the more it must insist on fallbacks: offline capability, distributed risk, transparent governance, and strong guardrails. Without them, a single bug or a single misguided policy could have nationwide repercussions.

But resilience is not only technical. It is institutional and cultural. It depends on contestability—the ability of citizens to switch service providers, to resist monopolies, to scrutinise change. It depends on pluralism—the coexistence of public and private rails, digital and physical media, centralised and decentralised systems. A healthy monetary ecosystem is not a monoculture but a landscape of options, each with its strengths and weaknesses, each offering a check on the others. The central question is not whether CBDC should exist but how it coexists.

Many readers will approach this subject with unease, shaped by headlines about surveillance or fears of coercive design. Others may arrive hopeful, believing that a digital pound could modernise social programmes, strengthen financial inclusion, or challenge entrenched intermediaries. Both instincts contain truth. What is lacking in public debate is a framework for distinguishing the possible from the probable, the desirable from the dangerous. This book aims to provide that framework. It will not answer every question in advance, but it will equip you to ask the right ones when new proposals emerge.

At its heart, the digital dollar dilemma—the digital pound dilemma, the digital rupee dilemma—is a story about choice, agency, and trust. It asks what freedoms we are willing to encode, what powers we are willing to delegate, and what safeguards we are determined to uphold. It forces us to grapple with the uncomfortable fact that technology amplifies whatever values we embed within it, whether noble or reckless. And it challenges us to design with an awareness of history: societies rarely intend to build systems that constrain liberty, yet they often drift into them through convenience, complacency, or crisis.

As you turn the pages ahead, you will encounter scenes of past monetary transformations alongside technical architecture choices, governance debates, and imagined futures. Each chapter forms part of a continuous enquiry: how can we harness the benefits of digital public money without sleepwalking into a system that narrows our freedoms? What protections are essential, what promises insufficient, what assumptions naive? What does "good" look like, not in brochure language but in constitutional terms?

The tension you should carry through this introduction is deliberate. The future of money is neither doom nor salvation. It is a crossroads. We stand at its edge not as passive observers but as participants whose decisions—technological, legal, cultural—will determine the next chapter of economic life. Whether the digital pound becomes an instrument of empowerment or a velvet clamp on everyday autonomy will depend on choices made now, before the code hardens, before the defaults become fate.

This book will not tell you what to fear or what to embrace. Instead, it will give you the means to discern. It will trace the lineage of money from physical artefact to programmable signal; expose the design levers that shape privacy, control, and resilience; outline the governance structures that separate democratic oversight from technocratic drift; assess the economic consequences for banks, households, and cross-border flows; and present plausible scenarios for 2035, from rights-respecting architectures to subtle but pervasive forms of soft coercion. Finally, it will leave you with a practical checklist—a way to evaluate any CBDC proposal in light of the values you believe a free society must uphold.

The stakes are high because money touches everything. It is the quiet infrastructure beneath our daily lives, the binding agent of markets, the medium through which we express choices, responsibilities, and solidarities. To redesign it is to redesign part of society itself. As we move deeper into an age in which code mediates more of our civic and economic experience, the question is not simply what CBDC can do but what it should be permitted to do. That debate belongs not only to experts but to every citizen.

The chapters ahead invite you to explore this terrain with curiosity, scepticism, and imagination. The digital future of money is approaching, and its contours are still malleable. The opportunity—and the responsibility—is to shape it with clarity, restraint, and a steadfast commitment to human dignity. The story begins with the simplest of transactions, but it ends with the principles that define a society.

Chapter 1
When Money Became Software

A century ago, in the dimly lit back room of a London grocer, families queued quietly to exchange their savings for notes and coins they could hide beneath floorboards. It was the early months of the Second World War, and rumours of bank failures travelled faster than official assurances. People wanted the weight of certainty in their hands: paper that did not require electricity, intermediaries, or permission. The grocer later recalled that it was the first time he had seen grown men tremble not from fear of bombs but from fear that the digits in their bank ledgers might evaporate.

Today, a different ritual unfolds. On the morning commute, thousands swipe open mobile wallets—faces illuminated not by danger but by dashboards of balances, instant transfers, and colour-coded spending histories. The trust that once rested on the solidity of paper now rests on silicon, encryption, and the hope that the infrastructure humming beneath our palms will behave as expected. Few of these commuters imagine the lineage that connects their casual tap to the wartime hoarder's frantic whispers. Yet both are acting on the same instinct: money is only as trustworthy as the medium that carries it.

This quiet continuity is often masked by technology's bravado. To many, the transition from coins to cards to digital wallets feels like a natural march of progress, a sequence of conveniences leading to an inevitable conclusion: money as pure code. But nothing about this evolution is inevitable. It is a story of changing ledgers—of what society chooses to record, who is permitted to record it, and who is authorised to verify the record. As we stand on the threshold of state-backed digital currencies, these choices surface again with acute clarity. The material form of money may have shed its physical body, yet its political and ethical weight has never been more evident.

This chapter is an attempt to peel back the familiar skin of everyday transactions and show the machinery beneath. It traces how money graduated from tangible token to intangible entry, from the bearer instrument in a pocket to a permissioned entry on a server. It asks how our behaviour changes when the medium changes—why people who once hoarded cash in tins now rely on mobile wallets that they cannot explain, and why each shift seems to tilt the balance of trust between citizens, banks, and the state. The transformation is not just technological; it is psychological and constitutional. Somewhere along the transition from paper to software, money ceased to be a thing and became a system.

That system rests, fundamentally, on ledgers. Not the dusty tomes of clerks but programmable, dynamic, ever-synchronising databases whose structure determines what is possible and what is forbidden. The ledger is the product. It governs privacy: which transactions remain shrouded, which leave trails. It governs speed: which transfers settle instantly, which linger unverified. It governs control: who may authorise, reverse, freeze, or scrutinise. When central banks propose CBDCs, they are not merely proposing new payment apps. They are proposing a new ledger for society—one that could consolidate oversight in ways unfamiliar to the traditional architecture of distributed banking.

Before we can debate the merits and risks, however, we need to understand what this new ledger *is*. What differentiates an account-based CBDC from a token-based one? Why should the average commuter care whether their digital pound is traced to their identity or validated like digital cash? Why does a transport subsidy that auto-expires tell us more about the future than a thousand policy briefs? These questions are not the purview of technologists alone. They shape the affordances of everyday life: the conditions under which salaries arrive, benefits update, or charitable donations remain confidential.

Consider, for example, the seemingly benign idea of a conditional payment. In programmable money, a payment can carry rules: it may activate only under specific conditions, remain locked until a defined moment, or be restricted to certain categories of use. A time-locked grant for a weekly bus pass may expire automatically if unused—a compassionate design to prevent administrative waste. Yet the same mechanism could be repurposed to shape behaviour subtly, steering or discouraging choices without any public debate. In the world of programmable value, intention is everything and assumptions are dangerous. What begins as a benign optimisation can harden into a silent form of policy.

These possibilities push us to confront what trust means once intermediaries fade. For most of the twentieth century, monetary trust was distributed across a network of banks, each holding partial responsibility for recording and reconciling balances. No single actor could see everything; no single failure could halt the entire system. It was messy, redundant, and occasionally inefficient, but it was plural. A CBDC, by contrast, risks concentrating trust in a single authoritative ledger maintained by the state. That concentration may bring efficiency, simplicity, and speed. It may also blur the institutional boundaries that historically acted as checks and balances on financial oversight. Citizens who once relied on a constellation of intermediaries may find themselves relying on a single, central arbiter—one whose decisions and failures have broader consequences.

The shift from distributed trust to consolidated trust is not inherently malign, but it is consequential. It raises questions about accountability and resilience: Who audits the auditors? What happens if the central ledger falters? How do we preserve transparency without sacrificing privacy, or gain speed without enabling overreach? These questions, once academic, now matter to anyone who pays rent, receives benefits, or navigates the growing interdependence between digital identity and digital money. In the world we are entering, the architecture of the ledger becomes a quiet constitution of economic life.

This chapter—the first major step into the heart of the book—invites you to examine the foundations of that constitution. It will not reduce money to abstraction but will draw you into its lived reality: the wartime hoarder clutching paper, the modern commuter trusting code, the policymaker debating the structure of a future ledger. You will see how choices at the technical level ripple outward to shape behaviour and expectations, subtly reforming the contours of trust.

And yet, this is only the beginning. As the chapter unfolds, the distinctions between account and token, between programmable and static, between distributed and centralised trust will gain sharper definition. You will encounter the possibilities that excite central banks and the dangers that ought to concern every citizen. You will see how a transport subsidy—mundane, almost forgettable—can illuminate the profound stakes of programmability. And you will confront the pivotal question that threads through the book: when money becomes software, who writes the rules?

The answers are complex, but the journey is essential. The nature of money has always shaped the nature of society. Now that money is shedding its physical form and becoming pure code, the stakes are greater than ever. The transition from paper to software is not simply a technical upgrade. It is a shift in power, perception, and possibility. As you continue into the chapter, you will see how deeply this transformation runs—and why understanding the ledger beneath your daily transactions may be one of the most consequential forms of literacy in the twenty-first century.

From paper IOUs to programmable value

On 3 September 1939, as Neville Chamberlain addressed the nation from Downing Street, people across London formed tense queues outside local branches of Barclays and Lloyds. In Whitechapel, a clerk later recalled how customers arrived with canvas bags and prams, withdrawing notes and coins to store at home. They feared that if war brought bank failures or restricted withdrawals, the digits recorded in ledgers might prove less dependable than paper held in the hand. That instinct—*trust the tangible*—was not irrational. It was grounded in experience, memory, and the simple assurance that a bearer instrument settles value without appeal to anyone else. They knew one truth. Money behaves differently when its form changes. Five words.

Eighty years later, near Liverpool Street Station in April 2019, commuters performed a contrasting ritual. Instead of clutching paper, they tapped screens, refreshed balances, and trusted invisible servers to settle every tap and transfer. Their confidence rested not on physical substance but on cryptography, layered networks, and the expectation that these systems would keep humming. Few paused to ask who maintained the ledger beneath the glossy interface or how that ledger shaped their economic freedom. Yet the shift from Whitechapel's hoarders to London's mobile-wallet commuters reveals the same quiet motif that runs through the entire history of money: trust migrates to the medium.

The movement from paper IOUs to programmable value is often presented as a natural evolution, a smooth arc from primitive tokens to digital sophistication. The truth is more jagged. Each shift in form changed not only what money *was*, but whom society trusted to verify it, store it, and honour it. More importantly, each shift altered behaviour. Wartime hoarders stacked coins because possessions felt safer than promises. Modern commuters swipe smartphones because code feels faster than cash. The medium nudges the mind long before it alters the law.

The earliest banknotes in Britain, issued by the Bank of England in 1694, made this shift explicit. They were IOUs—promises to pay gold or silver on demand. The public accepted them because they trusted the issuer, not the paper. But as deposits became entries in ledgers rather than claims on metal, the centre of trust moved again. By the late nineteenth century, household money increasingly lived as ink in account books. The object that mattered was no longer the note in one's pocket but the record maintained behind thick vault doors. What people trusted—often uncritically—was the institution's commitment to maintain an accurate ledger.

This arrangement survived because it distributed responsibility. A single bank failure could be catastrophic, but the system relied on many institutions recording, reconciling, and verifying balances. The ledger was fragmented. Control was plural. Even after the creation of central reserves, retail money remained a patchwork of private liabilities backed by collective regulation. Citizens relied on a network rather than a single authority. Trust was redundant by design.

Programmable value unsettles that arrangement. Instead of treating money as a claim on a bank or a physical token, it treats money as an object in software—a packet of code subject to rules. A conditional payment can be released only under specific circumstances. A time-locked transfer can activate at a fixed moment. A spending constraint can restrict where funds may be used. This is not hypothetical. Kenya's transport ministry demonstrated one version of this concept in 2020 when it trialled a bus-subsidy programme in Nairobi that loaded weekly allowances onto digital fare cards which automatically expired on Sunday evenings. The idea was pragmatic: avoid administrative waste, target benefits, reduce fraud. But it revealed a more profound reality. When money becomes programmable, design choices start shaping behaviour directly.

Contrast this with the wartime example. The 1939 queues showed citizens acting to preserve autonomy—hoarding notes to protect themselves from systemic shocks. Expiring subsidies reverse the direction of influence: the system guides citizens, not the other way round. In a programmable system, the *rules* travel with the money. Behaviour flows from architecture.

A common counter-example is Sweden's steady decline in cash usage. By 2018, many cafés and shops displayed *Inga kontanter tack*, signalling refusal to accept cash at all. Proponents argued that this shift showed society's comfort with immaterial money and its trust in digital payment rails. Yet the Swedish Riksbank warned in 2018 that such reliance concentrated systemic risk: a single technical failure could paralyse entire regions. This case reveals the tension that programmable systems cannot escape. Digital money may feel effortless, but it raises the stakes of infrastructure dependence. When the ledger is remote and unified, failure echoes widely.

To appreciate why these examples matter, we must recognise the centrality of the ledger. In the twentieth century, the ledger was a backstage instrument. Banks maintained records; customers rarely thought about them. But with programmable value—and with CBDC proposals—the ledger becomes the stage itself. It determines what transactions exist, what histories are visible, what permissions shape each movement of funds. Whether the ledger is account-based or token-based is not a technical footnote. It determines whether transactions are bound to identities or validated like digital cash; whether auditors see all flows or merely aggregated summaries;

whether citizens transact under conditions of oversight or under pockets of anonymity.

Account-based systems, long familiar to banks, treat each balance as inseparable from an identity. This strengthens compliance and clarifies liability. Yet it also turns the ledger into an instrument of visibility. The state or authorised intermediaries can observe flows with relative ease. By contrast, a token-based model, exemplified by certain digital-cash prototypes tested by the European Central Bank in 2021, allows value to circulate as objects validated cryptographically rather than by querying identity-bound accounts. Privacy improves, but so does the risk of misplacing tokens or exceeding transaction limits needed to deter illicit use. Here, again, behaviour bends to the medium. People cautious about surveillance choose tokens when offered. Others, seeking simplicity, prefer accounts. The ledger shapes incentives long before it shapes law.

What this transition reveals is a deeper phenomenon: the migration of trust. In Whitechapel in 1939, people trusted paper because it needed no permission to circulate. In Nairobi in 2020, riders trusted fare cards because they guaranteed predictable subsidies. In Stockholm in 2018, consumers trusted payment apps because merchants trusted them too. Each case shows trust settling in a different place—physical substrate, institutional promise, technical reliability. The medium acts as the anchor.

A limitation is worth acknowledging. Not all societies follow the same arc. In Germany, for example, cash usage remained above 70% of point-of-sale transactions in 2019 (Deutsche Bundesbank), reflecting cultural preferences for privacy and control. This is not simply nostalgia but a response to history—surveillance, inflation, and political upheaval leave marks on monetary behaviour. The German case tempers the narrative of inevitable digital dominance. Behaviour is culturally shaped, not technologically ordained. Yet even there, online payments surged during the COVID-19 pandemic, indicating that convenience and habit can erode longstanding patterns. The tension persists: digital systems rise, but attachments to bearer value endure.

If money's evolution were merely a matter of technology, we could treat these shifts as updates—improving speed, reducing cost, smoothing frictions. But money is constitutional. It structures relationships between citizens and institutions. It encodes who must trust whom. When programmable value becomes mainstream, these relationships change subtly but profoundly. A conditional grant is no longer a benefit alone; it becomes a rule. A time-lock is not merely a feature; it is a governance mechanism. A token is not simply a digital object; it is a statement about privacy and autonomy.

This coding of rules into money raises the question Whitechapel's hoarders never faced: what happens when trust must be placed not in the substance of money nor in the diversity of intermediaries, but in a single, programmable ledger maintained by the state? The answer is not predetermined. It depends on design, governance, and public consent. But the stakes are high because the ledger is no longer merely administrative. It is behavioural.

One motif anchors the thread through these examples: the *hand-off*. Wartime savers hoarded paper, hand-offs suppressed. Bank-led systems distributed trust, hand-offs delegated. Programmable value reclaims hand-offs at the code level. Money carries instructions from issuer to user, compressing the space for interpretation, resistance, or negotiation. The hand-off moves from human discretion to software enforcement. That movement is powerful. It can simplify public administration. It can narrow the room for fraud. It can also narrow the room for choice.

As we look back over this arc—from paper IOUs to digital ledgers to programmable value—one question persists beneath the surface: how much of our economic freedom depends on the *form* of money rather than its nominal value? This is not an abstract puzzle. It is a test for a century in which money is no longer a thing we hold but a system we inhabit.

The tension remains unresolved. When money becomes code, the challenge is not merely whether it functions but what it demands. Does the medium preserve the trust we place in it, or does it require us to extend trust further than we intended? The decision sits before every society poised to adopt programmable value. The trade-off cannot be wished away. It must be examined, compared, and faced.

The ledger is the product

On 20 October 2020, in Nassau, the Central Bank of The Bahamas switched on a system that made monetary history. The "Sand Dollar", a retail central bank digital currency, became available across the archipelago, promising faster payments, easier supervision, and better reach to distant islands. From the outside, it looked like a modern wallet scheme with QR codes and mobile apps. Inside, it was something more radical: a single, state-run ledger capable of recording, in real time, who held which units of national money and how those units moved. The centre of gravity for trust shifted. Citizens no longer relied primarily on a web of commercial bank records. They relied on a core ledger written and maintained by the central bank itself. The ledger never stays neutral.

That moment in Nassau captured the quiet truth of the CBDC debate. Most public conversations focus on interfaces, branding, or policy objectives: faster welfare disbursement, cheaper remittances, financial inclusion. Yet the decisive choices sit behind the screen. They concern how entries are stored, linked, and queried; who may see which slices of data; which actors can change the record; and under what safeguards. The ledger is not a technical afterthought. It is the product. It is the x-ray machine that reveals, or conceals, the skeleton of economic life.

The reason is simple and uncomfortable. Whoever designs the ledger decides what counts as reality. When a CBDC balance appears on a citizen's phone, it reflects a specific view into that reality: a set of tables, logs, and permissions that define what belongs to whom. If a transfer does not reach the ledger, it has not happened. If a transfer can be reversed at the ledger, it can be undone in life. The core system therefore determines three things at once: how private a transaction can be, how quickly it can settle, and who ultimately controls it.

Consider privacy first, not as a moral slogan but as a concrete pattern of visibility. In a traditional bank account system, the ledger is already powerful, but it is fragmented. A high-street bank in Manchester cannot see the full detail of a customer's spending at a bank in Milan. Regulators patch the gaps through reporting requirements and targeted requests. By contrast, a retail CBDC ledger held by a central bank could, by design, aggregate all flows across wallets and intermediaries. This is not a theoretical curiosity. The People's Bank of China, in its e-CNY pilots in Shenzhen and Suzhou from 2020 onwards, explicitly described a "managed anonymity" model: low-value transactions were pseudonymous at the user interface, but the central infrastructure still saw wallet identifiers and could, via telecom and bank data, reattach them to people when justified.

That architecture shows how ledger design shapes privacy. The same e-CNY wallet that feels as simple as tapping a card embodies a structural choice: a central node can reconstruct the full path of funds if rules permit. For citizens, this means that privacy exists not as an inherent property of the medium—as with cash—but as a function of policy choices about who may query the ledger and how often. The implication is stark. If the ledger maintains linkable histories by default, privacy can be narrowed silently through new access rules. If, instead, the ledger stores only what is necessary for settlement and relies on cryptographic proofs for oversight, the default bends towards discretion. The x-ray can be full-body or limited view.

The choice between account-based and token-based designs crystallises this tension. An account-based CBDC, like the prototypes explored by the Bank of England and HM Treasury in London from 2021 onwards, ties each balance explicitly to an identifiable user record. Transactions become movements between named accounts on the central ledger. This supports direct integration with tax authorities, social security systems, and anti-money-laundering controls. It also means that auditors and courts can, in principle, reconstruct an individual's entire transaction history with a few well-structured queries. For some policy goals, that clarity is intoxicating.

A token-based approach works differently. Units of value circulate as cryptographic objects validated by the ledger without continuous reference to a specific identity, closer to digital banknotes than to bank accounts. The European Central Bank's early experiments with "digital cash" in Frankfurt around 2020–2021, using techniques such as blind signatures, explored precisely this option: how to allow small-value, offline-capable payments that the central ledger could settle without learning who paid whom. Here, privacy is embedded at the structural level. Auditors might see aggregate flows or redeemed tokens, but they cannot reconstruct every coffee purchase or bus fare.

It is tempting to frame this as a straightforward trade-off between surveillance and anonymity. Reality is untidier. Token systems still leave traces at the device, wallet, or network level. If a hardware wallet is registered to a person and logs every token movement locally, the privacy gain can evaporate in practice. Conversely, account-based systems can incorporate strong safeguards: differential access for agencies, strict warrant requirements, and cryptographic techniques to minimise exposure. The ledger's design is necessary, not sufficient. The behavioural choices that surround it—who stores logs, how long they persist, how often they are queried—matter just as much.

Speed illustrates the same pattern in a different dimension. Real-time settlement is often presented as a headline benefit of CBDCs. Yet speed is not magic. It is the result of architectural decisions about how the ledger processes and confirms updates. The Bahamas Sand Dollar system, for instance, achieved near-instant payments across islands precisely because it centralised the retail ledger at the central bank while distributing wallet interfaces through regulated intermediaries. A transaction did not need to traverse multiple correspondent banks; it needed a single successful write to the core database.

That design improves one metric—time to finality—while constraining others. In a purely centralised ledger, every transaction competes for processing capacity at the same point. If volumes surge, as they might during a crisis, the system must either throttle some transactions or degrade performance across the board. By contrast, distributed account systems or some forms of token settlement can localise congestion. A failure at one intermediary does not freeze everyone. Once again, the ledger acts as x-ray and choke point simultaneously. The very property that makes it efficient also makes it fragile if redundancy is not built in.

Speed also has legal consequences. In a traditional card payment, settlement may take a day or more. During that window, disputes can be raised, fraud can be intercepted, or errors can be reversed before becoming final. A CBDC ledger that marks transactions as irrevocably settled within seconds reduces that buffer. Courts and regulators must then decide whether to allow administrative "rewinds" of the ledger under specific conditions or accept that finality means finality, even in hard cases. The core question is no longer purely technical. It is constitutional. Are we comfortable allowing a central authority to rewrite the ledger occasionally, or do we prefer to preserve reversible layers above it at the cost of some complexity?

Control brings these threads together. Control is not an abstraction. It shows up in observable decisions: who can freeze an account, who can impose limits, who can inspect records without consent, who can mandate upgrades. In a CBDC system, these powers are implemented directly at the ledger. If a court orders the seizure of assets, compliance is a function call. If a sanctions list needs to be applied, it can be encoded as a rule that the ledger checks before accepting each transaction. This can improve the enforcement of democratically agreed laws. It can also tempt policymakers to solve new problems through ledger rules rather than through open, contested legislation.

A credible counter-example comes from older real-time gross settlement (RTGS) systems. For decades, central banks have operated high-value payment ledgers—such as CHAPS in the United Kingdom or Fedwire in the United States—where settlement is centralised and final. Yet the public rarely expresses concern about mass surveillance or overreach in those systems. The reason is instructive. RTGS systems handle wholesale transfers between banks, not granular retail payments between citizens. The ledger's x-ray falls on institutions, not individuals. CBDCs change that scale.

They extend central-bank-grade recording into the daily lives of households and small firms. The underlying technology may be similar, but the social meaning is not.

For auditors, a unified CBDC ledger is a dream. It simplifies sampling, trend analysis, and fraud detection. For courts, it offers authoritative evidence: time-stamped, sequenced, cryptographically signed. For compliance teams, it reduces ambiguity about whether a transaction occurred. For citizens, however, the same clarity can feel like permanent exposure. Every mis-typed payment, every regretted purchase, every tentative donation leaves a durable mark in the official history of money. The question then is not whether the ledger records, but whether everyone should be able to see everything the ledger records.

Designers have tools to modulate this visibility. They can build layered access, where different actors see different views of the same underlying data; they can separate identifiers from transaction flows and require extra proof to reconnect them; they can store some information off-ledger and use cryptographic commitments to prove its integrity when challenged. Each choice, however, carries trade-offs. More privacy often means more complexity and potentially slower audits. More transparency often means higher risk of misuse or mission creep. There is no neutral setting.

One quiet motif runs through these choices: the *window*. An account-based CBDC with full transaction histories gives auditors a panoramic window onto economic life. A token-based system with strong privacy features gives them a narrower aperture, perhaps limited to aggregated flows, redemption events, or outlier patterns. Courts and regulators peer through these windows to make judgments; citizens live with the resulting level of exposure. The design of the ledger decides how wide each window opens and who gets a key.

It is tempting for technologists to describe the ledger as infrastructure—pipes, rails, neutral plumbing. That language is misleading. A CBDC ledger is closer to a constitution written in code. It allocates powers, defines defaults, and constrains behaviour before any human decision is made. Once deployed at scale, it is hard to amend without disruption. Interfaces can be redesigned, interest rates adjusted, and messaging campaigns refreshed. The core data model and access structure, by contrast, tend to endure. The ledger's first draft risks becoming the last.

This persistence creates a particular responsibility at the design stage. Choices about account versus token, centralised versus partially distributed validation, full histories versus minimised logs, all shape what future governments, regulators, and private actors can or cannot do. A central bank that embeds broad surveillance capabilities in its ledger and promises restraint relies on institutional virtue. A central bank that technically cannot see small payments without explicit escalation relies instead on structural limits. The former approach bets on character. The latter bets on architecture.

The unresolved tension lies here. If the ledger is the product, then the real question for any CBDC proposal is not "what can this system do for efficiency or inclusion?" but "what lasting windows does it open, for whom, and under what constraints?" Before a society accepts a new monetary x-ray, it must decide how much of itself it is willing to expose—and to whom.

Programmability 101

In October 2020, the People's Bank of China, working with the Shenzhen municipal government, distributed digital "red envelopes" of e-CNY to residents in a lottery-style trial. Shoppers could spend the new currency in designated stores for a limited period; if they did not use it by the deadline, the balance vanished from their phones. Merchants reported brisk weekend traffic as recipients hurried to tap and scan their way through the expiring windfall. The money carried instructions inside.

That small experiment in Shenzhen captured, in compressed form, the core idea of programmability. The units of value were not just entries in a ledger. They were scripted. They knew where they were allowed to move, by when, and for what purpose. Spend at a participating merchant within the time window, and the transaction cleared. Wait too long, or try to transfer the funds to another wallet,

and the system refused. The same yuan, issued by the same central bank, behaved differently because the code attached to it was different.
Programmability sounds abstract. In practice, it is as concrete as a countdown timer on a phone screen or a "declined" beep at a ticket barrier. When money becomes software, conditions can be attached to each transfer: only after a certain date, only before a certain deadline, only at certain types of merchant, only if other criteria are satisfied. Conditional payments, time locks, and spending constraints are simply three ways of expressing that fact. They are not exotic financial instruments; they are rules that travel with the money.

The simplest programmable pattern is the conditional payment. Show it by imagining a local authority that awards a £60 monthly transport subsidy to low-income residents via a CBDC wallet. The authority can express the policy as code: "Pay £60 to this wallet on the first of each month, *if* the citizen's income remains below a specified threshold and their residency status is unchanged." The payment is no longer a standing order that clerks must review. It is an automated decision: conditions met, value released; conditions failed, payment withheld. The rule is named explicitly in the system; developers encode it; the ledger enforces it. For administrators, this means fewer manual checks and fewer opportunities for fraud. For citizens, it means that a subtle change in data—an income record corrected, a residency entry misfiled—can instantly mute the flow of money.

Time locks build on the same logic. They define *when* a payment may move or *until when* it remains valid. A central bank might choose, for example, to issue emergency CBDC credits during a natural disaster that can be spent immediately but cannot be withdrawn or converted into other assets for thirty days. In software terms, every unit carries a timestamp and a simple rule: "Do not allow transfer to bank accounts before this date." The advantage is clear. Funds reach people quickly, but authorities gain confidence that the credits will support short-term consumption rather than be siphoned into speculative trades. The implication is equally clear. The right to decide when to hold, move, or transform value shifts away from the individual and towards the issuer's code.

Spending constraints narrow the field further by specifying *where* or *on what* value can be used. The Hong Kong SAR Government's 2021 Consumption Voucher Scheme, delivered through stored-value instruments such as Octopus cards and e-wallets, approximated this model: residents could spend vouchers at approved local merchants within set periods, but not use them to pay taxes, buy certain financial products, or shift funds overseas. Although that programme did not rely on a full CBDC, it showed how rules at the payment layer could steer behaviour. Programmable CBDC would bring those constraints closer to the monetary unit itself. Instead of a voucher instrument enforcing the rule, the core ledger could reject any transaction that did not match the allowed merchant categories.

A transport subsidy that auto-expires offers a compact example of all three concepts. Picture a city authority in Manchester issuing a £30 monthly CBDC subsidy to eligible residents for bus and tram fares. The payment is *conditional*: eligibility must be verified each month against current income and address records. It is *time-locked*: the subsidy appears in the wallet on the first day of the month and vanishes at midnight on the last if unused. It is *constrained*: the code permits spending only at registered transport operators' terminals, not at supermarkets or online retailers. What appears, to the passenger, as a simple "free travel balance" is, to the system, a small bundle of rules enforced automatically by the ledger.

The benefits are tangible. Administrators see reduced leakage: funds cannot be quietly diverted to unrelated purchases. Transport operators gain predictability: they know that subsidy payments settle instantly when a ticket is validated. Politicians receive metrics: they can measure uptake by route, time of day, or demographic group, and adjust policy with unusual precision. A visible behaviour emerges on the ground—more people using off-peak services, for instance, as the subsidy nudges them towards times with spare capacity. Efficiency becomes the sight of shorter queues at ticket offices and fewer complaints about missing payments.

But the risks are equally concrete. A resident whose income momentarily crosses the eligibility threshold due to an overtime shift might find the next month's subsidy withheld automatically. A migrant worker with patchy address records could watch credit vanish unused because they lacked timely information on how or when to redeem it. The same timer that encourages early use can create anxiety for those who struggle to keep track of deadlines. The system's tidy logic appears in human life as hurried trips, awkward workarounds, or resigned acceptance that some benefits will always slip away unused.

To see how deep the logic runs, compare programmable subsidies with unconditional transfers implemented on traditional rails. Finland's basic income experiment of 2017–2018, administered by Kela, paid a flat monthly sum to selected unemployed citizens via standard bank accounts. There were no conditions attached to how, when, or where recipients could spend the money; the only requirement was continued participation in the trial. Evaluations later emphasised psychological effects—reduced stress, greater sense of autonomy—alongside labour-market outcomes. That case, although limited and contested, illustrates an important limitation of programmability: more control is not always better. Sometimes, leaving money free to circulate according to recipients' own priorities creates benefits that rigid optimisation would miss.

Reconciling these examples highlights the motif that quietly threads through programmability debates: the *script* embedded in value. In Shenzhen, the script pushed people to spend quickly at approved merchants. In our Manchester subsidy scenario, the script channels travel behaviour while capping uncertainty for the budget office. In Finland's experiment, the absence of script was itself a design choice, signalling trust in recipients' judgement. Each case involves a decision about how much of social policy should be translated into code that fires automatically, and how much should remain in the sphere of human discretion, interpretation, and negotiation.

Conditional payments are not new in principle. Social welfare systems have long used eligibility tests and sanctions. What changes with CBDC-level programmability is the granularity and immediacy of enforcement. When a condition is monitored by caseworkers, there is room for context: a late form can be accepted, an error corrected, a local hardship recognised. When the same condition is monitored by a ledger, outcomes flip from "it depends" to "yes" or "no" in milliseconds. Every abstraction—"fraud prevention", "targeting", "behavioural incentives"—translates into a specific, observable pattern: a green tick on a device, or a blank line where funds once appeared.

Time locks, too, have analogues in the old world of paper cheques and fixed-term deposits. What distinguishes their programmable successors is their reach into everyday spending. A cheque that expires after six months is inconvenient; a digital grocery voucher that evaporates on Sunday night shapes weekend routines. Central banks have floated, at least as scenarios, CBDC designs that include interest rate tiers or expiry features to encourage spending during recessions. Even where such ideas remain hypothetical, their mere feasibility raises a question: if the script can change the velocity of money at the unit level, what guards are needed to ensure that macroeconomic nudges do not become microeconomic compulsion?

Spending constraints are perhaps the most visceral expression of programmability because they collide directly with people's sense of agency at the point of sale. A card that declines at a pub but works at a supermarket tells a story about someone's judgement. If that card is linked to a CBDC wallet, the story is written by the issuer. Some constraints may be widely accepted—preventing stolen or child-managed wallets from being used for gambling, for instance. Others would be far more controversial: blocking funds for political donations, restricting travel to certain regions, or throttling purchases in sectors deemed undesirable. The same code path that enforces a transport subsidy's boundaries could, without proper guardrails, enforce a government's preferences about lifestyle.

A counter-argument deserves fair hearing. Proponents of programmability point out that many such constraints already exist, implemented through merchant codes, sanctions lists, or contractual terms in private payment systems. You cannot use a standard debit card freely in every jurisdiction; you cannot buy certain goods online without identity checks; you cannot circumvent sanctions by relabelling a transfer. Programmability at the CBDC layer, they argue, simply moves these controls to a more transparent, inspectable domain. Rules written into a public ledger might actually be clearer and more contestable than opaque algorithms run by private networks.

There is truth in that claim. A well-designed CBDC could expose its scripts for public scrutiny, allowing citizens, journalists, and civil society groups to see exactly which conditions attach to which transfers. A transport subsidy's expiry rule, for example, could be published in plain language and audited by independent experts. This visibility would distinguish it sharply from present arrangements, where constraints are often buried in terms and conditions that almost nobody reads. Transparency, however, does not neutralise power. A clearly documented constraint can still be coercive if citizens lack meaningful alternatives or if changes can be imposed unilaterally through software updates.

The recurring motif of the script therefore returns with a sharper edge. Who holds the pen? Who decides when to revise the text? In systems where citizens can choose between multiple rails—cash, commercial bank money, regulated stablecoins, and CBDC—the impact of an objectionable script in one domain is cushioned by exit options. A resident can decline an expiring voucher and accept a slower, unconditional transfer instead. Where CBDC becomes the dominant or mandated rail, the script hardens. A rule once chosen becomes hard to escape.

At its best, programmability allows public money to behave more like a responsive instrument and less like a blunt one. It can make transport subsidies timely, emergency support automatic, and fraud detection more accurate. At its worst, it can make the rules of economic life feel like an invisible stage direction, guiding every step while leaving little room for improvisation. The transport subsidy that vanishes on the last day of the month is a small symbol of that duality: a neat solution for planners, a ticking clock for passengers.

The unresolved question is not whether conditional payments, time locks, and spending constraints *can* be implemented—they can, and pilots from Shenzhen to Hong Kong have shown how. The real test for any CBDC proposal is different: which scripts are society willing to embed so deeply into money that they execute automatically, and which scripts should remain at the level of policy, persuasion, or human judgement instead?

Trust after intermediaries

On a grey morning in September 2007, queues formed outside a branch of Northern Rock on Northumberland Street in Newcastle-upon-Tyne. News cameras caught pensioners clutching plastic bags of paperwork, young families with prams, and office workers on their phones, all waiting for the doors to open. The queue outside Northern Rock grew. The Bank of England had just announced emergency support for the mortgage lender. Technically, deposits were guaranteed. Practically, thousands of people decided they trusted their own judgement more than official statements and tried to withdraw their savings in cash. Trust in the institution had cracked; trust in the broader banking system survived, just. That scene is more than a story about panic. It shows how, for much of the twentieth and early twenty-first centuries, trust in money was distributed. Each bank kept its own ledger, subject to shared rules and backstops. When one institution failed, others could, and often did, continue to function. Central banks provided liquidity and oversight, deposit insurance softened the blow, and the web of intermediaries acted as a network of fuses. A failure at one node might be painful, but the entire circuit did not burn. The structure of trust was plural by design.

Proposals for retail CBDCs alter that structure. Instead of a mesh of commercial ledgers sitting on top of central-bank reserves, we contemplate a single, consolidated record of public money balances maintained by the sovereign. Intermediaries may still exist as wallet providers or service partners, but the decisive ledger—the one that determines who owns which unit of public money—sits at the centre. Trust after intermediaries becomes trust in the state's technical competence, institutional integrity, and legal constraints. The wiring diagram changes. So does the failure pattern.

To see the contrast clearly, it helps to look at how distributed trust has functioned in practice. When Lehman Brothers collapsed in New York in September 2008, the shock radiated through interbank markets. Confidence between institutions evaporated. Yet retail customers of high-street banks in Bristol or Birmingham still used cash machines, card terminals, and standing orders. They worried about the economy; they did not queue en masse to withdraw deposits. The architecture mattered. No single bank had a full picture of everyone's transactions. No single technical failure could switch off all retail money. The Bank of England's balance sheet served as anchor, but a multitude of institutions mediated everyday trust.

This distributed model carries costs. Every intermediary maintains systems, compliance teams, and capital buffers. Payments bounce between banks and schemes, creating friction. Supervisors must monitor dozens of entities, each with its own risk profile and incentives. Outages at one institution—say, a software failure at a major UK bank's online platform in 2012—may lock customers out of their accounts for days, even as other banks' systems operate normally. From a planner's perspective, the mesh looks messy. From a citizen's perspective, it offers redundancy. If one node fails, others remain available. The network of fuses protects against a total blackout.

A consolidated CBDC ledger promises a different picture: a single, authoritative record of balances and transfers. Show it in a hypothetical European context. The European Central Bank, in Frankfurt, runs a core CBDC engine. Commercial banks and payment firms across Paris, Madrid, and Tallinn connect their wallets and apps to that engine through standardised interfaces. When a citizen pays a shopkeeper using CBDC, the transfer is recorded once, directly on the central ledger, rather than bouncing between multiple intermediaries. The system reduces reconciliation overhead, shortens settlement chains, and gives policymakers a real-time view of payment flows. Efficiency appears as fewer failed transfers, faster clearing, lower back-office staff counts per transaction.

The name here is centralisation. The explanation is straightforward: by moving from many ledgers to one, the system removes duplication of effort and ambiguity about "who owes what to whom". The implication is double-edged. On the one hand, central banks can respond to stress with unprecedented clarity, seeing where liquidity hoards, where payment volumes spike, which regions suffer outages. On the other, that same clarity means the entire system depends heavily on a single technical spine. If the spine fractures—through cyber-attack, software bug, or operational error—the impact spreads everywhere.

We do not need to imagine the fragility of centralised financial infrastructure. High-value payment systems already embody it. When the Bank of England's RTGS platform experienced a significant outage in October 2014, property transactions stalled, corporate payments were delayed, and banks resorted to contingency measures. Retail accounts were largely unaffected because domestic card schemes and cash machines continued to operate on separate rails. The incident was serious but contained. A retail CBDC built on the same central engine would not enjoy that separation. The fuse box would sit much closer to ordinary households.

Modern distributed ledgers—of the blockchain variety—are sometimes presented as an antidote: trust dispersed across many nodes, no single point of failure. Systems like Bitcoin, first operating in January 2009, allow anyone to inspect the transaction history and verify balances independently. There is no central operator. Yet this model comes with different trade-offs: slower throughput, probabilistic settlement, governance by dispersed and often opaque communities of miners or validators. For a public authority responsible for national money, such a structure can feel too diffuse. The state cannot easily tune policy or comply with court orders in a system it does not control.

This is where CBDCs occupy an awkward middle ground. They are centralised in operation, yet they sit downstream of a long history in which trust was deliberately spread across intermediaries. They seek to keep the accountability of public money while borrowing the programmability and reach of digital rails. The quiet motif that runs through these choices is the *single switch.* With a distributed banking system, no single actor can, by itself, turn off all payments or see all details. With a consolidated state ledger, someone, somewhere, holds a switch that controls a far wider field.

The gains from such a switch are not trivial. An authority facing a bank run could, in principle, freeze only the affected institution's CBDC-linked wallets while keeping the rest of the system liquid. A government attempting to route emergency funds—during a flood in York, say, or a pandemic in London—could credit CBDC balances directly, bypassing intermediaries whose systems are down. Auditors could run real-time checks for anomalies, reducing undetected fraud. Legal enforcement could become faster; court-ordered asset freezes could take effect within seconds, not days.

Those gains reveal a different face when viewed from below. A citizen whose funds can be frozen centrally with one instruction experiences control differently from one whose money is spread across several institutions with different failure modes. Even if only extreme circumstances trigger such measures, the knowledge that they are technically possible shapes behaviour. People might keep more value in non-CBDC forms—cash, foreign currency, or commodities—if they fear arbitrary freezes. Or they might resign themselves to the convenience, hoping that constitutional safeguards will prevent abuse. Either way, trust pivots from a web of private intermediaries to a set of public guarantees about how the switch will be used.

Plural checks and balances do not disappear entirely in a CBDC world, but they move. Today, a citizen wronged by a bank error can escalate to an ombudsman, switch providers, or, in some cases, simply close an account and use another institution. Regulatory competition, while imperfect, disciplines behaviour. In a consolidated ledger, switching wallet providers does not change the underlying operator of the money. Complaints that ultimately trace back to ledger rules must be addressed at a higher level—parliament, courts, central-bank boards—where change is slower and more politicised.

A credible counter-example helps to ground the argument. Consider India's Unified Payments Interface (UPI), launched by the National Payments Corporation of India in April 2016. UPI created a real-time, interoperable platform through which banks and fintech apps could initiate transfers. From the user's perspective, UPI feels like a single rail; QR codes, phone numbers, or aliases all route to the same engine. Yet the underlying money remains commercial bank deposits, and multiple banks still compete to provide accounts and apps. UPI centralises messaging and switching, not monetary liabilities. It achieves speed and interoperability without fully consolidating the ledger of balances. This shows that digital efficiency does not automatically require the state to hold every retail record.

Reconciling UPI's architecture with CBDC proposals highlights the genuine choice faced by policymakers. They can aim for a "hub-and-spoke" model, where a public platform standardises connections but leaves liabilities and detailed records with banks. Or they can favour a "single spine" CBDC, where the state assumes responsibility for the core record of retail money. The first preserves more of the existing distribution of trust; the second reconfigures it sharply. The right answer is not purely technical. It depends on how much society wants the fuse box to remain segmented.

For researchers and practitioners, the critical behaviours to watch are small. How do people respond when a bank app goes down but a CBDC wallet remains up? Do they treat the public option as the ultimate safe harbour, shifting balances towards it in uncertain times and away from commercial banks? How do banks adjust their risk-taking and lending models if they know that deposits can migrate instantly to the central ledger? These behaviours will show whether distributed trust still plays a meaningful role or whether the consolidated ledger has become the dominant anchor.

Efficiency, too, must be measured in more than milliseconds. A system that processes payments quickly but generates political conflict or public suspicion may prove brittle. A distributed banking landscape that looks inefficient on paper may, in practice, provide social resilience by insulating citizens from single-point failures and policy shocks. Trust is not just a function of uptime; it is a pattern of expectations about how power will be used when things go wrong.

As CBDC designs move from white papers in Basel or London to pilot projects and then to possible deployment, the motif of the single switch will move from abstraction to lived reality. Who has access to it? What legal hurdles stand between a policy decision and a change in ledger rules? Can independent institutions—courts, parliamentary committees, privacy commissioners—see and constrain how the switch is wired? Or will those checks remain weaker than the technical capacity that has been created?

The unresolved tension is simple to state and hard to answer: how much distributed trust are we willing to trade for the convenience and clarity of a consolidated state ledger, and what concrete safeguards must accompany that trade so that the single switch never becomes a single point of failure for our economic freedoms?

Chapter 2
The Case for a State Digital Currency

On a damp Tuesday morning in Birmingham, a café owner named Aisha opened her till and counted the weekend's takings. The café had been full—families ordering breakfast, cyclists stopping in for tea, students tapping their cards as they dashed to lectures. Yet her bank balance told another story. Most of those card payments would not land for another forty-eight hours. A few would take longer. Fees would nibble at each transaction. Meanwhile, suppliers wanted paying today. Rent was due tomorrow. She wasn't short of customers; she was short of settlement. The lag between the tap and the cash flow was a gap she felt in her bones.

This gap is the quiet tax embedded in the plumbing of modern money. It is not captured in headline inflation figures or GDP growth rates. It is measured in overdraft fees, awkward phone calls with suppliers, stalled investments, and days spent waiting for what has already been earned. For millions of households and small firms, the problem is not access to money but the *pace* of money. Transfers hop between intermediaries, clearing houses, and batch processes long after the physical world has moved on. Aisha's dilemma is not dramatic, yet it captures the daily friction that any credible proposal for state digital currency must address.

Proponents of CBDCs often reach for abstract language—"efficiency gains", "payment modernisation", "public rails". But behind those phrases lies something human and immediate. A state digital currency, if designed with care, could deliver settlement that feels as natural as speaking: instant, certain, inexpensive. It could reduce the invisible drag that slows commerce and household budgeting alike. It could, in short, shrink the distance between effort and reward. And yet, as we will explore, speed alone is not reason enough to rebuild the foundations of public money.

The case for a CBDC begins to sharpen when we shift our gaze to the margins of the financial system—places where the private sector's successes are uneven, and its incentives misaligned with social need. Across the United Kingdom, one in eight adults struggles to access affordable digital banking services. Some rely on pay-as-you-go phones that buckle under the weight of bloated apps. Others face linguistic hurdles that make onboarding difficult. A not insignificant number live in areas where patchy mobile reception renders app-based banking unreliable. In these spaces, "financial inclusion" is not solved by opening yet another account. It requires infrastructure that functions even when devices are basic, signal is weak, or literacy is limited. It requires something more like a *public utility* for money.

Here, the promise of a state digital currency acquires moral force. Imagine a system that allows offline transactions for hours or days, enabling someone in a rural Scottish village to buy groceries during a storm without network coverage. Or a wallet that runs smoothly on older Android devices that many low-income households rely on. Or interfaces with language options that reflect the multilingual reality of Britain's cities. Such design choices are not bells and whistles; they are the difference between extending access and merely expanding account numbers. A CBDC cannot claim to foster inclusion if it assumes the bandwidth, devices, and fluency of the affluent.

The stakes become even clearer in moments of crisis, when the elegant theories of peacetime policymaking collide with tangled reality. When Storm Arwen struck northern England in November 2021, tens of thousands of households lost power for days. Bank branches closed. ATMs failed. Card terminals flickered out. Local councils struggled to distribute emergency funds through traditional channels. A state digital currency with offline capability and direct-to-wallet issuance would not have solved everything, but it could have provided a reliable means for governments to route relief funds immediately, even as the commercial banking system faltered.

At the same time, crises highlight uncomfortable trade-offs. Direct transfers require targeting. Targeting requires eligibility code. And eligibility code, unless carefully constrained, can creep into forms of conditionality that feel intrusive or paternalistic. How much information should a government be permitted to consult before routing emergency funds? How much should be embedded in the wallet's logic rather than left to human adjudication? These questions do not negate the value of crisis-ready rails; they challenge us to articulate guardrails robust enough to prevent technological capability from becoming a tool of overreach.

Yet perhaps the most compelling case for a CBDC arises not from the state's need to act, but from the market's need to be challenged. Britain's payment rails, though sophisticated by global standards, remain dominated by a small number of private actors. Card networks set fees that merchants quietly resent. Proprietary platforms decide which innovations flourish and which languish. The incentives of incumbents do not always align with the needs of the economy. A well-designed CBDC could serve as a public benchmark—an infrastructural baseline that private firms must outperform rather than rent-seek around. It could force innovation by its very presence.

This is not a call for monopoly. A state digital currency should not smother the creativity of fintechs or the agility of commercial banks. Instead, it should offer a floor: a fast, reliable, and reasonably private rail on which others can build. Competition would shift from who can extract the most fees to who can deliver the best services *above* the baseline. The existence of cash has long provided such a floor; nothing focuses the mind of a payment network quite like the knowledge that citizens can always walk away and pay with coins. A CBDC could update that discipline for the digital age—*if*, and only if, the system remains interoperable, optional, and governed by transparent rules.

The deeper logic behind these arguments returns us to a motif running throughout this book: money as infrastructure. When infrastructure fails, lives are disrupted. When it thrives, most people barely notice it. Today's payment infrastructure succeeds unevenly. It serves the digitally proficient, the urban, and the financially stable better than it serves the vulnerable, the remote, or the precarious. A state digital currency offers the chance—just the chance—to correct that imbalance by designing for the edges rather than the centre.

Still, enthusiasm must not obscure complexity. A CBDC cannot magically repair the social determinants of exclusion. It cannot replace the human judgement required in crisis response. It cannot, by itself, shift the cultural and commercial structures that shape how people use money. What it *can* do is create rails that lower barriers rather than raise them, rails that do not require the newest phone or the strongest signal, rails that keep functioning when profit incentives ebb. And by doing so, it can make the broader financial system more contestable, more accountable, and more resilient.

The paradox is that the most convincing argument for a CBDC is not that it delivers dazzling new capabilities, but that it delivers boring ones: transfers that arrive when needed; interfaces that work on modest devices; rails that survive storms; infrastructure that keeps private innovation honest. These are not glamorous selling points. They are the bones of a functional economy.

As you turn the page into this chapter, you will encounter the tensions that shape the case for a state digital currency: where speed becomes dependence; where inclusion becomes a slogan; where crisis response demands precision without coercion; where competition hinges on the presence of a public option rather than its dominance. And quietly beneath these threads sits the question that will determine the fate of any CBDC proposal: can we design public money that improves the fabric of daily life without narrowing the freedoms that make daily life worth defending?

Friction costs that citizens actually feel

On 12 July 2018, Visa Europe suffered a major outage that froze millions of card transactions across the United Kingdom for roughly ten hours. In Nottingham, a butcher named Martin O'Neill later told the *BBC* that he lost nearly a full day's takings because customers could not pay and many had no cash. His suppliers, however, still expected settlement on schedule. The failure lasted hours; the cash-flow effects lingered for days. A single technical fault at a private payment processor became, for small merchants across Britain, an unexpected credit shock.

The outage exposed a simple fact: the frictions embedded in modern payment rails are not abstract inefficiencies but lived discomfort. People feel them when rent is due, when a card terminal fails, when a refund disappears into the banking labyrinth, when thin margins buckle under settlement delays. Fees, lags, and reversals are not technicalities; they are the texture of financial life. And they persist not because the technology to remove them is absent, but because the incentives that shape private rails are misaligned with the needs of the people who use them.

To understand what a state digital currency could improve, we must first understand how these frictions arise at ground level. For small businesses, the first friction is time—*waiting* for money that has already been spent. A corner shop in Leeds that closes its till at 10 p.m. may see card receipts from that same evening arrive two or three days later, depending on the acquirer, the card scheme, and the settlement cycle. The shopkeeper sees customers come and go; her bank balance remains stubbornly static. The delay forces behavioural compensation: owners keep cash buffers, postpone supplier payments, or use overdrafts that accumulate interest. Time becomes cost.

Now name the mechanism. Settlement on card networks such as Visa or Mastercard travels through a stack of intermediaries: merchant acquirer, card scheme, issuing bank, and finally the merchant's account. Each step involves reconciliation. Each step introduces delay. It works—until it does not. During peak holiday periods, merchants in the UK reported 24–72-hour settlement times in 2019, sometimes longer when fraud checks were triggered. The process is reliable enough for routine commerce; it is unreliable enough to keep small businesses anxious. A CBDC rail, by contrast, would record the transfer directly on a central ledger, moving funds from payer to payee in seconds. The implication is not mere convenience. It is a structural shift in cash-flow management for millions of micro-enterprises.

The second friction is cost. Fees appear as innocuous percentages—1.5 per cent here, 2 per cent there—but for high-volume, low-margin businesses they bite hard. A bakery in Glasgow that sells £3 coffees and £2 pastries may pay up to £400 per month in card-processing fees, depending on volume. That amount is not the cost of ingredients, labour, or energy; it is the toll charged by payment intermediaries for moving numbers between ledgers. These fees fund legitimate expenses: fraud protection, network security, dispute resolution. Yet their opacity leaves merchants negotiating blindly. A state digital currency rail would not magically eliminate all costs; distribution requires infrastructure. But it could compress margins by reducing the layers between payer and payee. A transfer written once to a public ledger does not incur routing fees at every hop.

A third friction is uncertainty—the risk that a payment fails or reverses after the fact. Disputed card transactions force merchants into a dance known as "chargebacks". In 2020, retailers in the UK faced a surge in chargeback disputes as e-commerce volumes spiked, with some businesses reporting reversal rates above five per cent for certain product categories. Each reversal represents not only lost revenue but lost time: paperwork, evidence submission, and long waits for resolution. A CBDC settlement, when finalised on the ledger, would behave more like cash: immediate, irreversible, and immune to post-hoc disputes unless mediated through a separate legal process. The risk would not disappear; it would move to a different domain—courts rather than card schemes—and become more transparent.

But it is not only merchants who feel friction. Households face their own daily costs. A parent in Birmingham waiting for a Universal Credit payment may see funds "pending" for hours before appearing in their balance, even after the government has released them. A migrant worker in London sending money home through a remittance service may pay both a flat fee and a percentage, watching value leak away before the transfer even leaves the country. A commuter stuck in a queue at Euston Station when card readers glitch experiences friction as delay and embarrassment. In each case, the behaviour is visible: checking banking apps repeatedly, budgeting cautiously around uncertain timings, withdrawing extra cash "just in case". Friction breeds precaution.

To see the broader picture, contrast these frustrations with systems that have already reduced friction decisively. In India, the Unified Payments Interface (UPI), launched in 2016 by the National Payments Corporation of India, processes instant account-to-account transfers at scale. In May 2023 alone, UPI handled over eight billion transactions. Settlement is near-instant; fees are minimal. The ubiquity of QR-based payments has enabled micro-vendors—from fruit sellers in Mumbai to tailors in Jaipur—to accept digital transfers without worrying about multi-day lags. The system is not perfect; outages occur, and fraud attempts persist. But the behavioural shift is profound: people trust that a transfer sent is a transfer received.

Brazil's PIX system shows a similar pattern. Launched by the Banco Central do Brasil in November 2020, PIX accounted for more than 30 billion transactions within its first two years. Consumers embraced it for speed; merchants embraced it for cost. The fact that PIX is operated by the central bank is key: the incentive is not profit extraction but service provision. Both UPI and PIX demonstrate that when public authorities build instant, low-cost rails, private actors innovate atop them—wallets, budgeting tools, business dashboards. The rails matter because people feel their benefits directly.

A credible limitation must be acknowledged. Speed can amplify errors. A mis-typed recipient on PIX moves money instantly to the wrong person; recovery depends on cooperation, not an automatic reversal. In India, UPI disputes occasionally leave users waiting for days while banks coordinate. Instant settlement shifts risk from the intermediary to the sender. Settling with "cash-like finality" introduces a new kind of friction: user error hardness. Even so, the behavioural evidence speaks loudly. People choose speed over reversibility when the system builds trust through reliability. They prefer rails that behave predictably, even if the cost of mistakes rises.

This tension—between velocity and error correction—will shape any CBDC design. If the state offers instant settlement, it must decide whether to allow ledger rewinds (which undermine finality) or leave disputes to post-transaction adjudication (which may burden the courts). Neither choice avoids friction; each redistributes it. The question is where society prefers that friction to live: in the code or in human institutions.

Beyond merchants and households, the state itself faces frictions that CBDCs could ease. During the COVID-19 pandemic in March 2020, the UK government scrambled to distribute support to millions of employees and small businesses. Schemes like the Coronavirus Job Retention Scheme relied on existing banking rails, which buckled under unprecedented volume. Payments arrived late for some, early for others, and required extensive manual reconciliation. A direct-to-wallet CBDC transfer system could have provided a clearer, more uniform pipeline—eligible recipients credited instantly, without routing through intermediaries whose systems were never built for such surges. The implication is not that CBDCs are crisis cures, but that state systems benefit from rails designed for peak load rather than average load.

The recurring motif in all these cases is the *gap*—the gap between transaction and settlement, between expectation and reality, between effort and reward. A CBDC aims to close that gap by collapsing the settlement chain. Instead of funds ricocheting through private ledgers, they would be written once to a public, authoritative record. The gap shrinks. Behaviour shifts. Aisha in Birmingham receives her weekend takings on Monday morning, not Wednesday afternoon. Martin in Nottingham never loses a day's revenue to a card outage. The parent waiting for benefit payments sees funds appear when the state initiates them, not after clearing cycles run.

But another gap emerges, quieter and more constitutional: the gap between technical capability and institutional restraint. Instant settlement, if not carefully governed, can become instant freezing. Low fees can become a rationale for steering all payments onto the state's rails. Reducing friction cannot come at the cost of narrowing freedom. The more smoothly the rails run, the more tempting they become as default infrastructure—and the harder it becomes for citizens to move off them if policy changes in ways they dislike.

The question, then, is not whether CBDCs reduce friction—they can, and examples from UPI and PIX show how. The question is what we are willing to trade for that ease. Will the gap we close in economic life open a new gap in institutional power? Or can a publicly governed digital currency provide the texture of frictionless payments without eroding the buffer that intermediaries once provided?

The answer depends on design. And the design must follow a principle that no merchant counting a weekend's takings should ever forget: speed and certainty matter, but so does the freedom to choose rails that do not bind too tightly.

Financial inclusion or account expansion?

In January 2023, the Joseph Rowntree Foundation published a survey showing that nearly one million low-income adults across the United Kingdom had no reliable access to the internet at home. In Liverpool, a woman named Karen told researchers she routinely walked to a public library to check her Universal Credit account because her pay-as-you-go phone could not support the app. On days when the library shut early or the weather turned grim, she simply hoped that no messages had arrived. Her life was shaped not by the presence or absence of a bank account—she had one—but by the fragility of the digital tools that surrounded it.

The paradox is stark. Britain is a highly banked country: over 95 per cent of adults have an account. Yet millions still struggle to navigate digital finance safely and consistently. Phones crash. Data allowances run out. Interfaces assume perfect literacy. Rural signal drops without warning. The rhetoric of financial inclusion often celebrates account numbers as proof of progress. But inclusion is not an entry on a spreadsheet. Inclusion is whether someone can reliably use money when the network stutters, when language is unfamiliar, when devices are old, or when life is hard.

A state digital currency promises to widen access, but only if policymakers understand where exclusion actually sits. It does not sit in the absence of accounts. It sits in the canyon between *having* a financial tool and *being able to use it well.* That canyon runs through households, estates, small towns, and migrant communities—places where the vocabulary of "digital transformation" means little compared with the experience of a frozen screen or a declined purchase at the wrong moment.

One way to see the canyon clearly is to observe behaviour. In Bristol, a food-bank volunteer described how clients routinely borrow smartphones from relatives to authenticate payments. They queue, borrow a device, open an app, enter details, hand the phone back, and hope they typed everything correctly. This is not inclusion. It is an elaborate compensatory ritual. The name for what they lack is not an account. It is digital resilience: the ability to transact on one's own terms, regardless of device quality, network stability, or literacy.

CBDCs are often promoted as tools of inclusion because they can, in principle, be offered to anyone with a phone. But that assumption hides a problem. Phones age. Batteries degrade. Low-end devices buckle under the weight of modern apps. If a CBDC wallet demands constant connectivity, frequent updates, or rich graphics, it will exclude precisely those whom inclusion rhetoric promises to help. Design must start from real constraints rather than imagined users.

Take an instructive example. In the Eastern Caribbean, the Eastern Caribbean Central Bank launched DCash in March 2021. The system initially required users to register through a smartphone app. In Grenada and Saint Lucia, uptake lagged, particularly among older users and those with outdated phones. A major outage in January 2022—lasting nearly two months—eroded trust further. The system eventually returned, and features improved, but the lesson stood in plain view: a digital currency cannot expand inclusion if its technical demands exceed the capacities of the very communities least served by commercial banks. A sleek interface is not a gateway if the phone cannot run it.

Contrast this with Kenya's experience of mobile money. Safaricom's M-Pesa, launched in 2007, succeeded not because it offered sophisticated features, but because it worked on inexpensive handsets, required minimal literacy, and could process transactions through USSD codes even without mobile data. A farmer in Eldoret could send money during a blackout. A market trader in Kisumu could operate with a device costing under £15. The behaviour tells the story: people queued to deposit cash into their M-Pesa accounts because the service met them where they were, technologically and linguistically. The implication for CBDC design is unmistakable. Inclusion follows simplicity.

Offline capability is another frontier where rhetoric and reality often diverge. Policymakers speak enthusiastically about "offline access", yet few systems define what this means in practice. Does offline mean ten minutes without signal, or ten hours? Does it mean payments work between devices directly, or only after a delayed synchronisation? In rural Cumbria, where connectivity can vanish for entire evenings, offline capability must mean more than a token fallback. It must allow families to buy essentials while storms knock out cell towers. A household's experience—tap, beep, approval—must hold steadily even when the network does not.

Here, a useful comparison arises from Japan. Suica cards, operated by JR East and launched in 2001, enable stored-value payments across transport and retail. They do so without requiring live connectivity. The card and terminal exchange encrypted information directly, and systems sync later when networks permit. The experience is seamless. Travellers move through Tokyo's stations at speed. Crucially, the technology respects the limits of infrastructure. It succeeds because it anticipates failure. A CBDC that requires perfect connectivity is not an inclusive tool; it is an aspiration.

Language presents another barrier too often ignored. The UK's major cities host communities who speak Arabic, Somali, Polish, Urdu, Bengali, and more. A 2021 report by the Money and Pensions Service found that language or literacy challenges affected the financial confidence of more than two million adults. If a CBDC wallet launches with interfaces available only in English, or hides critical settings behind untranslated menus, it offers little more inclusion than a standard banking app. In London's Tower Hamlets, a Bengali-speaking resident faced eviction because she misunderstood an online rent-payment instruction during a period of interface redesign. The problem was not the technology itself; it was the failure to communicate plainly. Digital money only includes when its language includes.

A counter-example deserves acknowledgement. Estonia's digital-identity strategy, launched in 2002, is widely praised for seamlessness. Citizens authenticate securely across healthcare, banking, and government services. Digital literacy is high; broadband is widespread. For a country like Estonia, layering a CBDC on top of its existing digital infrastructure might indeed expand inclusion, because the underlying prerequisites—connectivity, devices, digital skills—are already distributed broadly. Yet Estonia's model rests on decades of investment and a population of 1.3 million. It cannot be transposed wholesale to larger, more diverse countries with uneven digital readiness. The limitation refines the argument: inclusion depends on context.

That context, in the United Kingdom, is mixed. Urban centres boast dense connectivity but deep linguistic diversity. Rural regions deal with intermittent signal and ageing devices. Many low-income households rely on second-hand smartphones with outdated operating systems. Migrant workers often juggle multiple apps across multiple countries, with no guarantee that a CBDC wallet would support cross-lingual verification. Behaviour reveals the truth: people work around their tools, not with them. They borrow phones, write passwords on scraps of paper, and avoid certain transactions for fear of making irreversible mistakes. These behaviours are not signs of financial irresponsibility. They are signals of design failure.

This brings us to the recurring motif that threads through inclusion: *access is not use*. A system may offer access in theory—download this wallet, open this account—but fail in practice when the user cannot operate it consistently. A CBDC that assumes high-end smartphones, stable networks, and fluent English will not close inclusion gaps. It will widen them. A CBDC that honours simplicity, tolerates offline periods, and respects linguistic diversity will not erase structural inequalities, but it will reduce the burden that poor design places on those least able to bear it.

Policymakers often measure inclusion by counting accounts. Yet accounts are merely containers. What matters is capability: the ability to transact at any time, in any neighbourhood, in any weather, without fear of technical collapse. True inclusion is visible in ordinary routines—a parent buying school supplies with an old handset; a pensioner paying for heating during a blackout; a migrant worker sending wages home without navigating byzantine menus. These are the scenes that define whether a digital currency serves society or merely expands the perimeter of formal banking.

The unresolved tension remains: will CBDC proposals in Britain and beyond treat inclusion as a lived condition or as a statistical achievement? And if inclusion is truly the goal, how will designers ensure that the first users of a state digital currency are not the affluent with new iPhones, but the citizens who most need tools that work when everything else falters?

Crisis rails and public interest payments

When Storm Arwen tore through northern England in November 2021, more than 200,000 homes lost power. In Northumberland, a shopkeeper named Susan kept her corner store open by candlelight, selling tinned food and bottled water to neighbours whose kitchens had gone cold. Yet she could accept only cash. Card terminals were dead. Mobile reception faltered. Several local bank branches closed for days because staff could not reach them. Residents who relied on online banking found themselves cut off at precisely the moment they most needed help. Councils scrambled to distribute emergency support, but eligibility checks clashed with the reality of downed networks. Money, the essential lubricant of crisis response, became as fragile as the power lines lying twisted across the roads.

The scene was not unique. The Texas winter storm of February 2021 knocked out ATMs for millions. After the Christchurch earthquake in 2011, New Zealand's major banks shut multiple branches for weeks, forcing the government to improvise cash-distribution schemes. In each case, the same paradox appeared: the more digital and interconnected a financial system becomes, the more brittle it can feel when infrastructure fails. Disaster strips away the luxury of multi-step transfers, batch processing, and high-bandwidth channels. What remains is a simple question: can a government get value into people's hands when intermediaries are down?

A state digital currency, if designed with crisis conditions at its core, could offer one answer. Direct-to-citizen transfers become technically plausible when the issuer controls both the ledger and the interface layer. But technical plausibility is not the same as practical reliability. Real resilience demands careful attention to targeting, eligibility, offline access, and institutional restraint. It demands an honest reckoning with what is gained—and what might be lost—when the state becomes capable of paying citizens directly with just a few lines of code.

To see how such a system could work, begin with the simplest behaviour: a government credits CBDC balances to wallets without routing through commercial banks. Show it through a concrete scenario. Imagine a flood in York disables multiple high-street branches while also disrupting regional data centres. If a CBDC system has been engineered with offline capability and distributed validation nodes, the Treasury could activate an emergency transfer—say £100—to every resident within designated postcodes. The ledger, structured for crisis mode, would accept and timestamp the transfers even if some nodes operate in degraded conditions. Recipients walking into a local shop could tap their devices or cards and complete a payment through offline protocols. The money would sync when networks returned. The implication is powerful: relief does not wait for the reopening of banks.

We have glimpses of this logic in recent history. During the COVID-19 crisis, Singapore deployed its Solidarity Payments in April 2020 through a mixture of direct bank transfers and cheques, reaching most households rapidly. But the system still depended on stable banking rails. In contrast, Nigeria's eNaira, launched in October 2021, was promoted as a channel for targeted welfare disbursement insulated from some commercial banking failures. Early progress was uneven—technical issues, limited adoption—but the ambition was clear. The state sought a rail that would not buckle if intermediaries faltered. These examples show the same pattern: governments search for ways to reach citizens without being hostage to fragile institutions.

Yet direct payments raise a thornier problem: *targeting.* Who should receive emergency funds? How should eligibility be determined when databases are incomplete or offline? The temptation is to embed targeting logic directly into the CBDC's code—release funds only to addresses flagged as affected; apply income filters; exclude those with outstanding sanctions. But these conditional rules, if embedded too deeply, risk turning the crisis rail into an instrument of bureaucratic precision at the cost of human judgement.

We can show this tension through experience. After Hurricane Katrina in 2005, the United States struggled to distribute aid quickly because eligibility systems were scattered and verification required multiple checks. Some residents waited weeks. Others received payments they were later asked to repay. A CBDC-like system might have solved the timing issue but exacerbated the fairness issue: a rigid eligibility script can deny help to those who fall between categories. A name misspelled in a database becomes a cold refusal at the point of need.

Japan's experience after the 2011 Tōhoku earthquake illustrates another trade-off. While the government disbursed cash support efficiently, municipalities relied heavily on local discretion—caseworkers, not algorithms, determined who needed urgent help. A CBDC system capable of direct transfers must find a way to preserve that discretion without sacrificing speed. The implication is clear: crisis rails must prioritise *inclusivity first, precision second*, or risk leaving the most vulnerable behind.

Offline access remains the sticking point. For a crisis rail to function, money must move even when networks fail. Here, we turn to Namibia's 2023 CBDC pilot, which tested low-bandwidth and offline prototypes for rural communities. Devices exchanged signed transaction records directly, storing them locally until they could reach a synchronisation point. The system was rudimentary but demonstrated a path: treat offline capability not as an add-on but as the backbone of emergency design. A family in a blackout-hit district should be able to buy bread with a tap, even if the nearest cell tower is out.

A credible limitation must be addressed. Offline protocols introduce risks: replay attacks, double-spending within small windows, device theft. Designers can mitigate these through spending caps, secure elements, or periodic revalidation, but each mitigation restricts ease of use. The more tightly the system guards against fraud, the less smoothly it may function in extreme conditions. Reconciling this demands humility. Crisis rails should focus on *low-value, survival-critical transactions* rather than large transfers, accepting minor inefficiencies to preserve human dignity.

Throughout these challenges, a quiet motif keeps emerging: *reachability*. Not in the technical sense of network topology, but in the human sense—whether the state can reach a citizen when systems fail. A digital currency designed for crisis must be reachable in three ways: the state must be able to reach citizens with funds; citizens must be able to reach goods; and communities must remain reachable to one another through exchange even when infrastructure breaks. Each layer requires different safeguards. Each demands design that assumes failure, not perfection.

Competition between public and private rails also plays a role. If a CBDC becomes the only reliable rail during emergencies, market incentives shift. Commercial banks may underinvest in resilience, knowing the state will provide a safety net. Payment companies may argue that maintaining redundant capacity is wasteful when a public system stands ready. Yet a CBDC should not become a monopoly by accident. Guardrails should ensure that commercial players remain accountable for their own robustness and that the crisis rail does not become the *default* rail. The state should be the backstop, not the everyday arbiter of payments.

An example of balanced coexistence comes from South Korea. During the Daegu COVID-19 outbreak in March 2020, the government issued prepaid "relief cards" and mobile vouchers that worked alongside private payment networks. The cards could be used even when certain digital services lagged, but they did not replace private options. The coexistence preserved contestability while ensuring reachability. A CBDC could mirror this model by positioning itself as infrastructure that only reveals its full power when private systems falter.

The hardest question lies in institutional restraint. Once a government has the ability to send money directly to every citizen, it may feel pressure to expand that capability beyond crisis contexts. The boundary between emergency relief and routine welfare may blur. The distinction between targeted support and behavioural incentives may erode. Code once written for exceptional moments may become the template for ordinary ones. The risk is not dystopian overreach but incremental normalisation. A society comfortable with direct-to-wallet emergency transfers may become comfortable with more frequent interventions that bypass intermediaries and public debate.

This is the unresolved tension at the heart of crisis rails. A CBDC can make emergency response faster, fairer, and more reliable—if designed with failure in mind. It can carry relief into blackout zones, bypass shuttered banks, and put autonomy back into the hands of citizens stranded by disaster. But it can also embed targeting logic too deeply, overconsolidate state power, and narrow the role of human judgement in moments when nuance is essential.

The question is therefore not whether crises justify direct-to-citizen payments—history shows they often do—but whether a society can design a system where the extraordinary remains extraordinary. How do we build rails that save lives in the darkest hours without allowing those rails to become the default pathways through which economic power flows every day?

Competition and innovation

On 16 November 2020, the Banco Central do Brasil switched on PIX, its new instant-payment rail. Within a week, more than 50 million Brazilians had used it. Within a year, PIX handles surpassed debit-card transactions nationwide. By 2023, street vendors in São Paulo were placing hand-written "PIX only" signs on their carts because transfers cost them nothing and cleared immediately. Major banks, long criticised for high fees, responded by overhauling their own apps, improving uptime, and accelerating settlement windows. PIX did not monopolise payments. It forced incumbents to compete.

Brazil's experience shows a simple pattern: when a public rail raises the baseline for speed and cost, private systems evolve. They either innovate or risk irrelevance. The question for countries considering CBDCs is whether a state digital currency could play a similar catalytic role—an infrastructural benchmark that pressures private rails to improve without smothering them. The question hides something deeper: what happens to innovation when the state itself becomes an actor with the power to set the floor of digital payments?

To understand the stakes, start with the behaviour of incumbents. When Visa Europe suffered its major outage on 1 June 2018, it revealed a vulnerability long understood by merchants but rarely acknowledged by the networks themselves: private rails can be efficient yet fragile. Competition, in theory, should compel redundancy and resilience. In practice, concentration dulls those incentives. When a few firms dominate card processing, the cost of building more robust systems often exceeds the competitive pressure to do so. A public rail—whether PIX or a future CBDC—disrupts that calculus by offering a credible alternative. If merchants can move transactions to a state-backed instant rail when reliability falters, private networks cannot rely on inertia.

The United Kingdom has seen faint echoes of this dynamic. Faster Payments, launched in 2008, accelerated account-to-account transfers from days to seconds. Banks initially resisted; some delayed adoption. But once the public rail gained traction, institutions scrambled to modernise. The behavioural shift was visible: customers stopped tolerating multi-day lags, and banks that lagged behind lost goodwill. The implication is direct: when a baseline improves, expectations shift. A CBDC, built with strict uptime guarantees and low fees, could deepen this shift.

Yet a credible counter-example complicates the story. Sweden's Swish system, launched in 2012 as a collaboration between major banks and operated by Bankgirot, became the country's dominant payment method without a state digital currency. By 2021, Swish accounted for more than 1 billion transactions annually. It thrived not because it competed with the state, but because banks cooperated under light public oversight to build something near-frictionless. Swish shows that private-led innovation can flourish when incentives align and when infrastructure—identity systems, mobile penetration, broadband—supports it. A CBDC is not the only path to competitive dynamism.

Reconcile this with the CBDC debate and a key insight emerges: public rails work best as *discipline*, not dominance. They set a floor that protects citizens and small businesses from exploitative fees, opaque rules, and sluggish clearing. They do not need to replace private rails; they need to give users the ability to *walk away*. The quiet motif threading through this subchapter is the *exit door*. Innovation thrives when exit is credible. A merchant who can switch payment channels with minimal friction disciplines the entire market.

Consider India. The Unified Payments Interface (UPI), though not a CBDC, functions as a public digital rail that reshaped the competitive landscape. When UPI launched in 2016 with instant, low-cost transfers, private wallets such as Paytm and PhonePe pivoted rapidly, enhancing features and tightening security. Banks upgraded their apps. Fintechs layered credit, budgeting tools, and micro-insurance atop UPI rails. The ecosystem did not stagnate; it flourished. And crucially, UPI did not extinguish alternative options—NEFT, IMPS, cards, and wallets all endured. Innovation flowed precisely because no single actor, public or private, held all the pipes.

A CBDC could act similarly if designed with openness as a founding principle. Open APIs, non-exclusive access for fintechs, and interoperability across wallets would allow private actors to use CBDC balances as a substrate on which to build services—budgeting tools, loyalty programmes, subscription management, sector-specific apps. The CBDC becomes plumbing; private creativity becomes architecture. But if a CBDC system restricts access or privileges a narrow set of intermediaries, the opposite occurs: the state rail becomes a bottleneck, freezing innovation rather than accelerating it.

Another behavioural dimension matters. Consumers gravitate towards systems that "just work". Reliability is innovation's unsung engine. A state-backed CBDC, if engineered with rigorous stress testing, could set a gold standard for uptime. That standard exerts competitive pressure. If a bank app goes dark during a holiday shopping rush, but the CBDC wallet remains operational, users may shift balances. If settlement on private rails takes hours while CBDC settles in seconds, loyalty erodes. These shifts are small individually. Combined, they can move markets. Private rails then must commit more investment into resilience and user experience simply to retain their customer base.

Yet there is a danger. If the CBDC rail becomes too attractive—free, instant, ubiquitous—private firms may not compete but retreat. Why invest in alternative systems if the state rail absorbs most volume? Why build redundancy when the public infrastructure already dominates? The result could be dependency rather than diversity. Here, the limitation becomes clear: a CBDC designed without guardrails may crowd out innovation by accident.

Guardrails should therefore focus on boundaries. The state should set standards, not extract rents. It should operate the core ledger, not the user interface layer. It should allow unlimited innovation on top, while refraining from embedding commercial features inside the CBDC wallet. The public option should be a narrow, neutral rail—not a super-app. This design principle mirrors the architecture of the internet: TCP/IP enabled billions of creative possibilities precisely because it did so little.

An instructive example lies outside finance. The European Union's requirement for number portability, introduced in 2003, allowed consumers to retain mobile numbers when switching providers. Competition accelerated. Prices fell. Service quality improved. The regulation did not force users onto a state telecom provider. It created an exit door that disciplined private firms. A CBDC can create similar pressure by ensuring that payments are portable across wallets and providers, severing the lock-in effects that often suppress innovation.

A second example comes from the UK's Open Banking initiative, launched in 2018 after the Competition and Markets Authority's investigation into banking competition. By mandating standardised APIs, the UK effectively turned bank accounts into interoperable platforms. Fintechs flourished. Incumbents responded with better apps, streamlined onboarding, and smart budgeting features. Open Banking shows that competition emerges not from the state displacing private firms, but from the state setting rules that prevent incumbents from suffocating newcomers. A CBDC, with open programmability parameters and transparent access rules, can extend this logic to payments.

The unresolved question sits at the intersection of efficiency and pluralism. A CBDC can raise the baseline. It can force private rails to modernise. It can correct market failures and reduce rents. But will it preserve the incentives for private actors to experiment, fail, and reinvent payments? Or will the gravitational pull of a state-backed rail prove too strong, drawing the market into a stable but stagnant centre?

The answer may lie in the design of the exit door. Can users switch between CBDC rails and private rails without friction? Can fintechs build services atop CBDC balances without permission bottlenecks? Can merchants choose pricing models that encourage competition rather than channel lock-in? And most importantly: can the state commit, in architecture as much as in law, to remaining the floor rather than the ceiling?

Chapter 3
The Risks We Cannot Outsource

Late one autumn evening, a schoolteacher in Edinburgh opened her banking app to reconcile monthly expenses. Buried among the routine entries—groceries, bus fares, donations to a local food bank—she noticed a transaction highlighted in amber. The payment was hardly remarkable: £25 sent eight months earlier to a civil liberties group after a peaceful march. What unsettled her was not the amount but the new label appended to it: *review pending under updated compliance criteria*. Nothing about her behaviour had changed. What had changed was the rulebook applied retroactively to her past. A protest donation, legal then and legal now, had acquired a different shade of meaning because the system that processed it had been silently reinterpreted. The transaction remained hers. Its significance did not.

This quiet re-labelling is a distilled version of a broader dilemma. As money becomes software, the past becomes editable—not in the sense of altering the transaction itself, but in the sense of altering its context, its classification, its risk score, its visibility to agencies and algorithms. A centralised digital currency amplifies this power. A single, persistent ledger—one capable of linking hops across wallets, devices, and time—turns private patterns into public artefacts. Even the most benign activity can acquire unwelcome resonance months or years later, depending on who queries the ledger and under what mandate. The risk is not dramatic abuse but cumulative reinterpretation: routine life reclassified line by line.

The promise of CBDCs often rests on efficiency, inclusion, and resilience. Yet the shadow side of that promise lies in the quiet mechanisms through which control can tighten without overt legislation. A digital wallet that updates overnight may change default spending limits, activate new behavioural nudges, or embed compliance tools that alter the incentives of daily life. A crisis-response feature, introduced for emergencies, may linger and evolve. A debugging function may become a surveillance vector. Software updates are mundane until the moment they are not. And when the wallet is the citizen's main interface with public money, even a subtle change can ripple outward with constitutional force.

To appreciate the stakes, consider the contrast with cash. When a storm sweeps across a region or when systems fail, cash reveals an old-fashioned virtue: graceful degradation. Notes still circulate. Coins still buy essentials. No update can render them temporarily unusable. No central server can flick them off. By comparison, a CBDC built atop a single ledger—however robust—becomes a point of concentration for risk. Cyber-attacks, insider errors, software bugs, or targeted interference can disrupt not just a bank or a card processor but the very medium of everyday exchange. The physical world absorbs shocks slowly; the digital world can fail fast.

This fragility intersects with another, quieter threat: *soft controls*. Not outright prohibitions—those attract scrutiny and political resistance—but small, plausibly deniable restrictions. Spending caps tightened "for safety", temporary freezes framed as "security reviews", nudges steering citizens away from particular merchants "pending verification". In isolation, each friction is modest. Combined, they create a behavioural ambient pressure. People become cautious about transactions that feel scrutinised, even when lawful. They hesitate before donating, travelling, or purchasing goods that might place them in ambiguous categories. It is the soft edge of power, where control is exercised not through force but through subtle engineering of choice.

Across these risks runs a common motif: *the boundary of control.* Not merely who controls the ledger, but who controls the interpretation of the ledger; not merely who can freeze funds, but who can classify funds; not merely who can secure the system, but who can switch it off in the name of security. These boundaries are political as much as technical. They determine whether CBDCs enhance public trust or erode it, whether citizens experience digital money as empowerment or constraint.

The chapters that follow trace four threads. First, the question of total recall: what it means when every hop becomes linkable and every link becomes a potential liability. We examine how retrospective rule changes can turn yesterday's ordinary payment into tomorrow's flagged anomaly, and how societies might limit such reinterpretation. Second, we turn to the quiet power of wallet updates—how silent changes to client software can reshape incentives overnight, and why due process must extend into the realm of code. Third, we confront the fragility of centralised digital infrastructure, placing CBDC resilience alongside cash's old but durable virtues. And fourth, we explore the slippery terrain of soft controls, where spending throttles and social spillovers can chill lawful behaviour without ever declaring themselves instruments of punishment.

Throughout, the goal is neither alarmism nor resignation, but clarity. Sovereign money carries sovereign responsibilities. Some risks cannot be outsourced to algorithms, intermediaries, or foreign platforms. Others cannot be mitigated through efficiency alone. A society that chooses to embed its monetary life in a programmable system must decide how that system will treat dissent, error, misidentification, inconvenient generosity, technical failure, and human imperfection.

As you enter this chapter, the question waiting beneath each page is simple and unsettling: if we build money that remembers everything, updates itself silently, reacts instantly to commands, and embeds guardrails we cannot easily see, how much of our economic autonomy survives the transition? And if autonomy is to endure, what forms of restraint must surround a system powerful enough to reshape daily life with a single push of code?

Total recall finance

On 3 February 2022, the Royal Canadian Mounted Police (RCMP) issued an order instructing financial institutions to freeze dozens of accounts linked to the Ottawa convoy protests. Some freezes targeted recent transfers. Others reached back weeks. One donor in Toronto, who had contributed a modest amount through a crowdfunding site in January, discovered her bank card declined at a supermarket checkout after the rule change. Her donation had been lawful when made. It became actionable only after the category of "suspicious" was updated. The payment had not changed; the interpretation had. The past had been reclassified.

The episode was temporary, controversial, and eventually unwound. But it illuminated the central dilemma of total recall finance: when every hop is linkable and every record permanent, the meaning of a transaction is never fully settled. A CBDC, with its consolidated ledger and built-in analytical capacity, magnifies this tension. The power to search, filter, and relabel grows as the data grows. What begins as compliance can drift into reinterpretation. What begins as metadata can calcify into judgement. And what begins as a single flagged donation can become a pattern inferred, a character sketch drawn from numbers alone.

To grasp the significance of this shift, start with the behaviour that makes total recall possible: persistent linkability. When a CBDC ledger records transfers with fine-grained identifiers—even pseudonymous ones—each hop accumulates context. Show this through a simple chain. A student in Manchester pays £15 to a bookshop. The bookshop pays a local printer. The printer pays a supplier abroad. The ledger encodes these motions as separate lines, but analytical tools can stitch them together, cluster them, and tag them. The name for this practice is transaction graph analysis. The explanation is straightforward: link enough hops and you map a life. The implication is not merely privacy loss; it is behavioural vulnerability.

A real-world analogue already exists. Since 2014, the United States Treasury's Financial Crimes Enforcement Network (FinCEN) has employed large-scale pattern analysis across Suspicious Activity Reports. Banks submit data; algorithms flag anomalies. Yet the system remains fragmented. One institution sees only a slice of a customer's financial world. A CBDC collapses these slices into a single vantage point. The state does not need to request data. It already has the ledger. This structural shift creates a qualitative change: surveillance can become ambient rather than episodic.

Consider another checkable example. China's e-CNY pilots, rolled out in Shenzhen from October 2020, introduced what officials described as "managed anonymity". Low-value payments appear pseudonymous at the interface, but wallet identifiers and telecom data can be linked when necessary. This model preserves some privacy for everyday use, yet it leaves the structural capacity for total recall intact. The ledger sees everything; policy decides what to expose. The behaviour this enables is subtle. A purchase today may be benign. Six months later, under a new regulatory campaign, it may fall into a flagged category. A system designed for efficiency becomes a system capable of retrospective reinterpretation.

A credible counter-example complicates the picture. Estonia, since 2002, has built one of the most transparent digital governance frameworks in the world. Every state database query must be logged. Citizens can review who accessed their information and why. Abuse is punished. This oversight regime demonstrates that linkability does not automatically yield misuse. Strong procedural guardrails can temper structural power. Yet Estonia's success depends on exceptional institutional trust and a small, digitally literate population. Scaling such safeguards to larger, more diverse nations with complex political ecosystems is not straightforward. The limitation clarifies the argument: technical capacity must be matched by institutional maturity.

Here a quiet motif emerges: *the shadow archive.* A CBDC ledger becomes an archive not just of payments but of inferred meanings. Every transaction sits in a long corridor of metadata—time, location, device, merchant code, wallet version. Such metadata may lie dormant for years until a rule change, investigative sweep, or analytical model activates it. A £25 donation to a civil liberties group, like the Edinburgh schoolteacher's example, may pass unnoticed until a risk model update casts it in a new light. The shadow archive does not accuse; it categorises. It does not punish; it prioritises. Yet categorisation can shape life as surely as coercion.

To see why, examine how classification systems operate in adjacent domains. In April 2023, the UK Financial Conduct Authority updated its guidance on "high-risk third countries". Banks promptly reconfigured their monitoring systems. Transfers previously treated as ordinary became subject to enhanced scrutiny. Customers heard from compliance teams. Some faced delays. The underlying behaviour—sending money to relatives—had not changed. The classification had. This is the logic of total recall: the ledger supplies the material; policy supplies the frame.

Extend this logic to a CBDC. A new policy on "sensitive gatherings" could require retrospective analysis of transactions near protest sites. A change in rules around charitable donations could trigger reviews of past contributions. A tightening of foreign influence regulations could reclassify overseas subscriptions. None of this requires malice. It requires only the normal bureaucratic impulse to update criteria. The risk stems from accumulation: when all flows are linkable, classification changes propagate across years of data in seconds.

Linkability also alters citizen behaviour through anticipation. People start to imagine how their economic past may be interpreted by unknown future authorities. This is the behavioural counterpart to total recall. A journalist may hesitate before funding an investigative outlet abroad. An academic may think twice before paying membership fees to an activist network. A nurse may reconsider donating to a politically sensitive cause. The hesitation is not paralysis. It is calibration. And calibration, repeated across millions, reshapes civic life.

Critics may argue that audits and warrants remain safeguards. Yet warrants assume a world of discrete requests—access sought for a specific target. A CBDC ledger enables continuous oversight without overt access events. The risk model itself becomes the watcher. And risk models do not sleep. They classify at scale, flag anomalies at speed, and operate in the grey zone between policy and practice.

Supporters counter that machine analysis can also protect citizens by detecting fraud, identifying financial abuse, and strengthening anti-money-laundering efforts. These benefits are real. Data can save lives, prevent exploitation, and support vulnerable individuals. But benefits do not neutralise risks. They sharpen the question: what constraints should limit retrospective reinterpretation? Should past transactions be immune to new rules unless authorised by a court? Should certain categories of payments—political donations, medical services, legal advice—receive enhanced privacy? Should retention windows be limited? How does a society balance analytical power with democratic accountability?

Return to cash for perspective. Cash forgets. A £10 note exchanged at a charity stall carries no tag. A coin dropped into a collection bucket records nothing of motive or identity. Cash's forgetfulness protects both anonymity and ambiguity. It preserves the right to act without being permanently inscribed. A CBDC's memory, by contrast, is perfect unless deliberately constrained. Its permanence makes total recall possible; its programmability influences how that recall is exercised.

One further motif underscores the danger: *policy drift*. A rule created for a narrow purpose can expand. A freeze category designed for urgent counter-terrorism may broaden to include politically ambiguous organisations. A reporting requirement intended for large transfers may be lowered over time. A data-sharing agreement adopted in crisis may persist in calm. Drift is rarely declared. It accumulates quietly, justified by efficiency or security. The ledger, once built, becomes the path of least resistance.

A hypothetical illustrates the practical stakes. Imagine a CBDC system that initially restricts its high-scrutiny analytics to transactions over £5,000. After a high-profile financial scandal, the threshold lowers to £1,000. After a political controversy involving small-scale crowdfunding, the threshold lowers again. Overnight, millions of ordinary transactions fall into enhanced analysis. No new law is passed. No debate is held. The shift occurs through internal policy updates and algorithmic adjustments. The citizen experiences only the outcome: more flags, more questions, more second looks.

The unresolved tension is this: how does a democratic society harness the legitimate advantages of linkability—fraud detection, public-interest auditing, safety—without slipping into a regime where every financial gesture becomes a shard of a permanent, reinterpret-able record? What limits must bind the shadow archive? And what legal, technical, and cultural commitments are needed to ensure that tomorrow's rules do not retroactively turn today's ordinary life into a map of suspicion?

Policy by wallet update

On 9 January 2018, Apple publicly confirmed that a software update released the previous year had quietly slowed performance on older iPhone models. The intent, Apple said, was to prevent unexpected shutdowns. Many users saw something different: a unilateral change that altered how their devices behaved without notice, choice, or clarity. Lawsuits followed in the United States and the United Kingdom; regulators demanded explanations. The episode was not about speed alone. It was about power—who decides when a device changes, and how transparently that decision is communicated. It revealed a truth that matters far beyond smartphones: silent updates do not simply fix bugs; they reorganise incentives and reshape behaviour.

A CBDC wallet, unlike a phone, would sit at the heart of economic agency. If its software can change overnight, without visible debate or meaningful consent, policy itself can shift overnight. A tweak to transaction-ordering rules could slow some payments and accelerate others. A revised risk-scoring module could nudge users away from certain merchants. A new spending cap, pushed through as a "security enhancement", could throttle behaviours deemed inconvenient. What Apple inadvertently illustrated, a state digital currency could institutionalise: policy delivered not through legislation but through code deployment.

To understand how these changes manifest, we must begin with a simple behavioural fact: users rarely read update logs. They accept new terms, click "Agree", and move on. Show this through a concrete case. In April 2022, PayPal updated its Acceptable Use Policy in the United States. Overnight, users awoke to headlines claiming the company could fine them $2,500 for spreading "misinformation". PayPal quickly walked back the clause and called it an error, but the damage was done. People closed accounts, charities voiced alarm, and legislators demanded clarity. The mechanism was not sinister—it was procedural. A clause slipped into an update without robust internal review. The implication is clear: silent changes, even accidental ones, can cascade into distrust when the stakes involve money.

A CBDC wallet update carries far greater gravity. Unlike PayPal, it would not be just one service among many. It would be the principal interface for sovereign money. A change to its code is therefore a change to public infrastructure. And yet, without binding safeguards, such changes could be pushed as quietly as any app update. The wallet becomes a policy surface. The update becomes a policy act.

Consider a hypothetical based on real dynamics observed in digital payments. A government implements a nightly update enabling automatic rejection of payments to merchants with unresolved compliance flags. Perhaps the intent is protective. Overnight, however, wallet users in a coastal town find that their local fishmonger's payments fail because a batch of KYC documents expired over the weekend. Customers blame the shop. The shop blames the wallet. The wallet blames the update. Behaviour changes instantly without a single law amended. The act was technical; its consequences are civic.

This pattern echoes earlier experiences with payment platforms. In October 2010, WikiLeaks faced coordinated financial blocks from Visa, Mastercard, and PayPal after US government pressure, despite no formal legal action at the time. Transfers to the organisation failed without warning. The platforms updated rules internally; users discovered only when their payments bounced. The episode showed that control exercised through software and policy updates can be faster and more far-reaching than control exercised through courts. That is the core risk for CBDCs: the faster the update, the thinner the due process.

To see how silent updates might work in a CBDC context, examine the structure of client-side software. Modern financial apps use remote configuration files—JSON manifests, feature flags, and rule sets—to toggle behaviours without requiring a full download. These mechanisms allow developers to react to fraud spikes or outages within minutes. Show this through a pragmatic example: in February 2023, several UK fintechs deployed remote rule changes to mitigate waves of authorised push-payment fraud. They tightened transaction thresholds, added friction steps, and rerouted suspicious payments. Most customers never noticed the shift; they simply encountered an extra prompt. The technique worked operationally. But it also demonstrated how easy it is to shape transactions without public debate.

A CBDC wallet with similar architecture could adjust parameters instantly: offline spending limits, merchant category permissions, transaction velocity caps, dispute flow rules. Policies could be trialled on subsets of users, A/B tested, then rolled out universally. The wallet becomes a laboratory; citizens become data points. The technical explanation is simple. Remote configurations allow granular control. The implication is constitutional: policy becomes provisional, experimental, quietly mutable.

A credible counter-example offers a measure of hope. Estonia's digital identity infrastructure, built from 2002 onwards, requires agencies to publish public logs of every access request. Citizens can see who queried their data, when, and for what declared purpose. This logging regime constrains silent changes because updates that alter behaviour leave footprints. Abuse is detectable. Yet even Estonia does not push constitutional policy changes through client apps; it separates code maintenance from rule-making. The limitation clarifies the path: transparency must be structural, not optional.

Threading through all these dynamics is a motif: *the silent switch*. It is not the kill switch of dramatic fiction but the quiet toggle buried in configuration files—the setting that changes how the system behaves long before the citizen realises it has happened. A silent switch can reorder transaction priority, change anomaly thresholds, or alter who qualifies for micro-incentives. Small shifts accumulate. Over months, they can remake the behavioural environment of a population.

To illustrate, imagine a CBDC pilot in Manchester. At launch, the wallet offers a modest cashback incentive for public transport use, encouraging greener behaviour. Months later, an update lowers the incentive from 5 per cent to 1 per cent for budgetary reasons. Users notice, grumble, and move on. Then another update introduces time-of-day restrictions: no rewards for peak travel. Then a further update removes cashback altogether. None of these changes require legislation. The incentive environment has been re-engineered through client-side updates alone. Behaviour shifts not because Parliament debated it but because a file changed.

The democratic risk is not only the speed of change; it is the asymmetry of knowledge. Policymakers and engineers understand the new rules before citizens even see the prompt. The wallet carries its own logic, evolving under the bonnet. Without meaningful notice and version transparency, people cannot contest what they cannot see. Nor can courts adjudicate policies that never formally surface.

To mitigate these risks, societies would need principles akin to software constitutionalism: mandatory public version histories, binding notice periods for non-emergency changes, and a legal distinction between bug fixes and behavioural modifications. Even emergency patches must be subject to retrospective review. Without such guardrails, the CBDC wallet could become an instrument whose most consequential changes occur late at night, during updates no one remembers approving.

The unresolved question lingers beneath every example: if public money becomes programmable money, and if programmable money evolves through client updates, how can a democracy ensure that monetary policy, civil liberties, and daily economic incentives are not quietly rewritten in the space between one software version and the next?

Cyber resilience and kill switches

At 2:17 p.m. on 7 October 2023, the Swedish payments processor Bankgirot experienced a cascading outage that halted salary disbursements, bill payments, and merchant settlements across Stockholm. Pharmacies could not verify subsidies; some supermarkets accepted goods on trust; commuters queued at ticket machines that refused digital cards. The malfunction lasted only a few hours, but the ripple was immediate: ordinary life slowed, tense, waiting for a system reboot. Bankgirot restored service by evening, yet the episode exposed a truth Sweden rarely has to confront. A payments system designed around speed and centralisation can fail fast. Cash, sidelined but still present, quietly absorbed the shock.

Notes passed hands. Coins bought essentials. When the servers stopped, money carried on.

The scene is instructive because it marks the edge of a deeper tension. A central bank digital currency promises resilience—modern cryptography, high-availability data centres, and rapid failover protocols. Yet it also concentrates risk. A CBDC ledger, especially if unified, sits at the heart of national economic life. A vulnerability is not a local glitch. It is a systemic event. And such events do not wait for the most convenient hour.

Outages, attacks, and insider errors are familiar hazards in the digital world. What changes with a CBDC is scale. A compromised retail bank slows a portion of the economy; a compromised sovereign ledger slows the whole. The fragility is architectural, not moral. Technical excellence mitigates risk; it cannot annihilate it. Which raises a simple, disquieting question: what happens when the central nervous system of public money is forced into silence?

To explore this, start with a visible behaviour: what people do when digital rails stall. During the Bank of England's CHAPS outage on 20 August 2014, solicitors delayed high-value property transactions, car dealerships halted deliveries, and small businesses reverted to scribbled IOUs. The Bank restored service the same day, explaining the fault as a corrupted code path. The incident was brief yet revealing. A single malfunction created a backlog of £289 billion in unsettled payments. The lesson is concrete: outages do not merely inconvenience; they freeze temporal commitments. A CBDC with retail reach would extend such freeze risk into millions of micro-transactions.

The first major claim concerns exposure to state-level attacks. Show it through a documented case. On 12 May 2017, the WannaCry ransomware attack crippled the UK's National Health Service, forcing hospitals to divert ambulances and cancel appointments. The malware spread through outdated Windows systems, not through financial rails. Yet it demonstrated how quickly a coordinated digital assault can paralyse critical infrastructure. The name is evocative but the mechanism mundane: attackers exploited unpatched vulnerabilities and moved laterally across networks. The implication for a CBDC is clear. A nation-state adversary with motivation and sophistication could target the validation layer, the identity service, or the telemetry systems of a centralised ledger. Even if funds remain intact, temporary paralysis would disrupt economic life.

A contrasting example shows what resilience can look like when systems are designed around decentralised redundancy. In 2012, the Icelandic financial services infrastructure suffered a cyber-attack that targeted card processors. Merchants switched to cash. Emergency supplies were distributed. Because cash remained widely circulated, transaction flow never fully halted. The episode illustrated the virtue of graceful degradation: a system that slows under stress rather than collapses outright. Cash does not require synchronised clocks, correct signatures, or network consensus. It simply moves.

The second claim concerns insider error—the overlooked threat. Complex financial systems often stumble over the simplest mistakes. In June 2021, a single Deutsche Bank employee accidentally sent $6 billion in a routine processing mishap. Internal controls caught the error in time, but the incident exposed how automation and human oversight can misalign. In a CBDC context, an insider error affecting ledger validation rules or revocation logic could ripple instantly across wallets. The behaviours at stake are both technical and human: misconfigured permissions, hasty deployments, a poorly tested patch. The implication is structural: a centralised ledger collapses the safety margins that normally arise from institutional plurality.

A credible counter-example offers constraint. Singapore's MAS (Monetary Authority of Singapore) has repeatedly demonstrated rigorous stress-testing of financial infrastructure. Its November 2022 simulated cyber drill involved dozens of institutions and tested coordinated incident response under severe attack conditions. The model works because Singapore couples centralised oversight with distributed operational responsibility. Yet even MAS acknowledges that centralised digital currencies introduce "novel concentration risks". The limitation matters. Strong governance reduces fragility; it cannot neutralise the architectural realities of a single ledger.

Threaded throughout is a quiet motif: *the kill switch.* In digital systems, kill switches are not dramatic levers; they are lines of code—failover triggers, emergency revocation tools, global freeze functions. They exist for good reasons: containment, fraud mitigation, crisis stabilisation. Yet they can also be misused, misconfigured, or invoked under ambiguous authority. A kill switch embedded in a CBDC wallet ecosystem could freeze a class of transactions, a category of merchants, or even a region's wallets during perceived instability. A technical safeguard becomes a governance pivot.

Show the dynamic with a behavioural example. Imagine a cyber-attack targeting a major metropolitan transport network, causing payment anomalies. Engineers identify suspicious transaction sequences and activate a kill switch on affected merchant categories "pending investigation". Overnight, commuters cannot pay for rail tickets. The initial aim was containment. The lived outcome is economic paralysis. The motif surfaces again: single-ledger fragility magnifies the effects of well-intentioned actions.

The third claim concerns visibility. A CBDC ledger records not only balances but timing, routing, signatures, and device attestation. During an outage or attack, engineers and authorities must examine logs, reconstruct states, and apply patches. This increases operational speed but narrows margin for error. Compare this to the behaviour observed during India's 2016 demonetisation. The policy decision was controversial, but the mechanism revealed something important: physical money, even when scarce, does not require recovery protocols. It simply re-enters circulation when conditions stabilise. Digital money, by contrast, must reconcile. Reconciliation under stress is brittle.

A limitation must be acknowledged. Not all centralised systems fail catastrophically. Visa's 1 June 2018 outage across the UK and Ireland disrupted millions of transactions, yet the network restored partial functionality within hours and full service shortly after. Incident reports cited a hardware switch malfunction. Visa's redundancy absorbed much of the shock. But the episode still produced a concrete metric: 5.2 million failed transactions. The system did not collapse, but neither did it degrade gracefully. Cash and alternative rails filled the gap, again showing the importance of pluralism.

As we consider CBDCs, the core question becomes architectural: should sovereign digital money rely on a singular ledger, or should resilience be built from layered redundancy—offline-capable wallets, local settlement modes, and fallback tokens? Without such layers, kill switches become all-or-nothing tools. A bug becomes a national event. A hack becomes a sovereign emergency. A misconfigured rule becomes a population-level disruption.

The quiet motif returns: the kill switch is only as benign as the moment that triggers it. Which authority invokes it? Under what thresholds? With which oversight? Is the invocation logged, reviewable, reversible? These questions are not procedural; they are constitutional. They determine whether resilience serves citizens or merely centralises vulnerability.

We end in tension because the tension is real. If cash represents graceful degradation—slow, local, imperfect but enduring—then a CBDC represents rapid synchronisation—efficient, elegant, and exposed. How, then, should a society choose between speed and independence? And can a single ledger for public money ever avoid becoming the kill switch it was designed to prevent?

Shadow bans and soft controls

On 15 April 2021, Singaporean taxi drivers began reporting a strange pattern. Riders using certain credit cards found their payments delayed or declined near nightlife districts. Banks later acknowledged that new anti-fraud algorithms had been activated overnight, raising risk scores for transactions in specific merchant categories. Nothing illegal had occurred. No regulation had changed. Yet drivers lost fares, riders walked home, and businesses complained of a sudden chill. The city had not imposed a ban. Software had imposed friction.

This small disturbance captures the essence of soft controls: measures that do not prohibit conduct but shape it through subtle impediments—an extra prompt, a temporary hold, a reduced limit, a "pending review" message that appears without explanation. These frictions seldom rise to the threshold of public controversy. They rarely appear in legislation. They live in the grey zone between policy and engineering, where intentionality becomes ambiguous. Did someone choose the rule? Did the model infer it? Who can see when a limit is applied? The visible behaviour is simple: a payment slows. The invisible logic is where power resides.

A CBDC intensifies this dynamic. A unified ledger allows precise enforcement of spending categories, velocity limits, and recipient permissions. When combined with fine-grained identity attributes, the system acquires the capacity to throttle behaviour without issuing an outright denial. A transaction that would once clear instantly may surface a warning: "Additional verification required." Another may proceed but count towards a weekly cap. A third might succeed only after a cooling-off period. None of these actions is dramatic. Each shapes conduct.

To understand how small frictions influence behaviour, consider China's documented experiments with social credit between 2014 and 2020. While often exaggerated in Western commentary, the programmes did produce concrete measures. In 2018, the National Public Credit Information Centre reported that individuals on certain blacklists were denied 17.5 million flight bookings and 5.5 million high-speed rail purchases. The mechanism was not violence or prosecution; it was automated disqualification. A digital system quietly withdrew privileges. The behaviour at stake was economic participation. The implication for CBDCs is not that such controls will be adopted wholesale, but that the architecture could support equally granular interventions.

A counter-example offers nuance. During the COVID-19 lockdowns of 2020, New Zealand's payment systems showed remarkable restraint. Banks hesitated to enforce merchant-category restrictions even when fraud risk increased, emphasising public continuity over algorithmic hygiene. Soft controls were avoided. This demonstrates that institutional norms can inhibit technological possibilities. Yet it also underscores a limitation: restraint is cultural, not structural. It relies on goodwill, not on guardrails.

Thread through these cases a recurring motif: *the invisible handbrake.* Not the classical metaphor of markets, but a digital mechanism that slows behaviour without announcing itself. The handbrake appears as a delay, a prompt, a reclassification, a cap. It does not immobilise. It merely drags.

The first major claim concerns sector-specific caps. Show this through a practical scenario. Imagine a CBDC designed with spending tiers to reduce financial crime. Transactions at high-risk categories—pawnshops, gambling venues, unregistered remittance points—trigger protective friction. The policy is well-intentioned. But classification is fallible. A legitimate pawnshop in Birmingham that serves low-income households may find itself marked as high-risk due to historical data quirks. Customers discover that their CBDC payments require additional verification. Some give up. Others shop elsewhere. The shop's revenue dips. The behaviour changes, not because of law, but because of an algorithmic label inherited from another context.

Named example: in 2015, Barclays tightened monitoring of money-transfer operators after regulatory pressure. Somali remittance firms in London faced account closures. Legitimate family transfers stalled, creating hardship documented by Oxfam (2016). No criminality was alleged. The throttle emerged from risk classification. The implication for a CBDC is sharper: throttling could occur not at the level of banks but at the level of wallets—embedded, automatic, and invisible.

The second claim concerns spillovers from scoring systems. Consider South Korea's 2020 credit-scoring reforms, which incorporated telecoms payment histories. The intention was inclusion. Yet some consumers found their scores suppressed due to late phone bills unrelated to actual creditworthiness. The behaviour affected was mundane: bill timing. The implication is structural: when multiple datasets feed a scoring engine, arbitrary linkages can contaminate outcomes. A CBDC with integrated identity services could inadvertently replicate such spillovers. A late utility payment might influence transaction scrutiny. A high volume of cash withdrawals might flag a wallet for "enhanced monitoring". Users adapt their behaviour to avoid triggering scrutiny—even where no wrongdoing exists.

A credible limitation tempers alarm. The European Central Bank's 2022 CBDC privacy study explicitly rejected social credit linkages, stating that any integration of behavioural scoring would violate EU law. This demonstrates that policy design can prohibit spillovers. Yet it also emphasises that the safeguard is legal, not technical. If political winds shift, the architecture remains capable of supporting different choices.

The third claim concerns cumulative friction. Behavioural economics offers a clear metric: small impediments reduce participation. Show it with an academic reference. A 2013 study by Shah, Mullainathan, and Shafir demonstrated that minor logistical barriers—such as multi-step processes—sharply reduce uptake of beneficial programmes among low-income households. Replace these barriers with financial friction and the pattern persists. Each extra click, delay, or verification prompt disproportionately affects those with limited time, data access, or cognitive bandwidth. A CBDC that introduces frictions unevenly risks entrenching inequality under the guise of safety.

The motif of the invisible handbrake appears again when examining merchant throttling. In March 2022, several UK fintechs began quietly blocking payments to crypto exchanges for "consumer protection". Some banks forced customers to call hotlines to override defaults. Others capped monthly transfers. These measures were well-intended attempts to reduce fraud. Yet they also created de facto gatekeeping. A citizen's lawful transaction encountered friction not declared in law. With a CBDC, where the wallet is both payment tool and regulatory surface, such measures could scale across millions overnight.

A deeper risk arises when throttles are selective. If certain neighbourhoods, professions, or demographic groups become subject to heightened scrutiny—whether due to historical fraud patterns or algorithmic bias—soft controls morph into quiet forms of discrimination. A 2020 audit led by the US National Institute of Standards and Technology found that facial-recognition error rates were disproportionately higher for non-white populations, affecting authentication in payments and identity contexts. Imagine such biases embedded in CBDC access controls. Authentication failures translate into slowed transactions, repeated prompts, or temporary freezes. The behaviour is technical. The social effect is unequal.

A counter-example illustrates mitigation. Brazil's Pix system, launched in November 2020, added optional per-user caps after a wave of express kidnappings. But the caps were adjustable and transparent, allowing users to reset limits as needed. The policy avoided blunt social spillovers. This shows that, with design care, friction need not become coercion. Still, Pix relies on existing bank intermediaries rather than a single sovereign ledger; CBDCs compress these layers, raising stakes.

Throughout these dynamics runs a quiet tension: friction accumulates quietly. No single throttle seems alarming. But frictions stack. A flagged merchant here, a reduced limit there, an extra prompt elsewhere. The aggregate effect is behavioural conditioning. People learn which transactions "feel smooth" and which "feel risky". They optimise for smoothness. And smoothness becomes a proxy for acceptability.

This conditioning produces a civic consequence. Lawful activities that fall into ambiguous categories—journalism, activism, cross-border remittances, politically sensitive donations—may attract more friction. Individuals noticing delays or prompts may adjust behaviour to avoid bureaucratic irritation. A journalist steps back from funding a source. A student refrains from donating to a controversial cause. A migrant reduces remittances because each attempt triggers extra steps. Nothing is banned. Everything is nudged.

The unresolved question sits at the centre of this subchapter: if soft controls can shape behaviour without public scrutiny, how does a society distinguish between justified safety measures and imperceptible coercion? And if the boundary between friction and freedom is drawn in code, who ensures that the invisible handbrake remains a safeguard rather than a tool for silent governance?

Chapter 4
Architectures: Account, Token, Hybrid

On a grey spring morning in Tallinn, a café owner taps her phone against a battered card reader. The payment fails. She tries again. Still nothing. A moment later, she shrugs, reaches into the till, and hands the customer their change in coins. The café hums on, indifferent to the glitch. The reason is simple: she trusts the system, but she does not rely on any single version of it. Cash, cards, mobile apps, local bank transfers—each offers a different path to the same outcome. The architecture of money is plural, and because it is plural, it is resilient.

Now imagine removing that plurality. Imagine the same transaction depends on a single national ledger, a single wallet interface, a single design philosophy. Would the café owner wait patiently for the reader to reconnect, or would she find that the payment system's architecture has quietly enlarged the stakes of a simple sale? When we speak of digital money, we tend to focus on features—speed, convenience, programmability. But architecture is destiny. The decisions buried in code and protocols determine what a society can do when things go right, and what it must endure when things go wrong.

A central bank digital currency forces that destiny into sharper relief. It is not just money made digital; it is money reimagined. Whether the system relies on accounts tied to verified identities, tokens that circulate like digital cash, or hybrids that split responsibilities between central banks and private providers, these choices shape the balance between privacy and oversight, resilience and centralisation, innovation and uniformity. Architecture defines who asks permission, who grants it, who sees what, and who carries blame when the rails fail.

The debate often begins with the most intuitive model: account-based CBDCs. Here the logic is clear. A wallet maps to a verified person, balances sit on a trusted ledger, and access is granted according to roles: citizen, auditor, regulator, court. Compliance becomes elegant. Audit trails are crisp. Tax reconciliation can be automated. Yet clarity has a cost. Identity-bound systems are the antithesis of cash. They reveal more than they hide. Every transaction becomes a small confession: where you were, what you paid for, perhaps even why you paid. The gains in transparency are matched by losses in anonymity. And once privacy thinning becomes a default, it is difficult to reverse.

The alternative—token-based CBDCs—carries its own paradoxes. Tokens promise something close to digital cash: transferable without identity, spendable hand-to-hand, resistant to tracking. But digital cash faces a stubborn challenge that paper never had: double spending. Preventing it requires some intermediary—algorithmic or institutional—to validate uniqueness. Tokens that depend on real-time validation are cash-like only in metaphor. Tokens that avoid validation risk fraud. Limits and revocation, essential for public safety, undermine the bearer quality that gives tokens their intuitive appeal. Creating digital cash that behaves like physical cash is not impossible. But it is fraught. Design choices echo through the entire system.

Between these poles lies the hybrid model, now a favourite among central banks. In this arrangement, the state maintains the core ledger while private institutions distribute wallets, authenticate users, and provide services. The structure mirrors existing two-tier systems where commercial banks interface with citizens and the central bank anchors the monetary base. Hybrids promise operational scalability and political acceptability. They spread liability. They preserve a measure of competition. Still, the architecture remains centralised at its core, and centralisation carries obligations. If the base ledger falters, the entire ecosystem trembles. Citizens may not care who manages which layer. They care that the tap of a phone or the scan of a code simply works.

Yet the most revealing question is not what happens when systems perform perfectly; it is what happens when they fail. Digital payments fail more often than we admit: network outages, cloud misconfigurations, certificate expirations, distributed denial-of-service attacks, software regressions. Cash never fails in this way. A frayed note remains spendable. A coin does not require synchronisation. Digital money must be designed to degrade gracefully. Without offline-first capabilities—secure elements that store value locally, QR-based vouchers that work without connectivity, mesh networks that synchronise when power returns—a CBDC becomes brittle. The architecture must bend, not break.

The chapter you are about to enter sits at the intersection of engineering and civics. It asks how a society chooses the rails on which its economic life runs. It explores what an identity-bound architecture reveals or conceals; what a token system protects or endangers; what hybrid models promise or complicate; and what offline resilience means for millions whose livelihoods depend on the quiet reliability of daily transactions. Architecture, here, is not about diagrams or protocols. It is about power, constraint, and the lived experience of money.

As we move deeper, one question will surface repeatedly: when a country builds a CBDC, what exactly is it building—a tool, a channel, a memory, or a boundary? And if architecture shapes freedom as much as function, which trade-offs will society accept, and which must remain non-negotiable? Only by understanding the bones of the system can we judge the body that grows around it.

Account model: clarity with strings attached

On 28 October 2020, Estonia's Tax and Customs Board announced that it had automatically pre-filled income declarations for more than 94 per cent of residents, drawing on real-time employer reports submitted through its long-running digital infrastructure. Within hours of filing season opening, thousands of citizens received precise reconciliations, refunds, and notifications without speaking to an official or calculating a figure. The system worked because every earnings record was tied to a verified identity, lodged in a state-run account framework, and accessible under tightly defined roles. What looked effortless in the interface was enabled by a deeper architecture: the account model as an organising principle for public finance.

This scene captures the promise—and the sting—of an account-based CBDC. Identity-bound balances create clarity. They also create exposure. The same precision that allows automatic reconciliation of tax obligations also enables fine-grained visibility of personal transactions. Efficiency deepens. Privacy thins. An account architecture does not forget, and it does not blur.

The first major claim begins with that visible behaviour: a system that knows exactly who you are and what balance belongs to you. Estonia's model shows how identity-based rails can streamline state functions. *Show*: a citizen logs in and sees a pre-populated tax return derived from verified employer deposits. *Name*: Estonia's e-Tax system (launched 2000) integrates employment, social insurance, and banking data. *Explain*: because each payment originates from an authenticated account tied to a legal identity, reconciliation becomes deterministic. *Implication*: a CBDC using a similar structure could deliver instantaneous tax adjustments—precision at scale—yet sacrifice informational discretion that cash currently preserves.

A parallel comes from the United Kingdom's 2003 introduction of PAYE Real Time Information (RTI). Employers began submitting wages data every pay cycle, enabling the government to adjust credits and deductions dynamically. The behaviour shifted: citizens increasingly experienced taxation as ambient rather than episodic. Yet this model remains partially decentralised; employers, not a central monetary authority, provide the inputs. A CBDC compresses these layers. Once the central ledger becomes the settlement source for wages and transfers, the informational pathway narrows. The authority that reconciles is the same authority that records.

The second claim concerns role-based access—an architectural feature that promises constraint but can broaden quietly over time. Consider how the UK's Serious Fraud Office, under the Criminal Finances Act 2017, gained the ability to issue Unexplained Wealth Orders, compelling disclosure of financial records. The power is targeted and warranted, but its operation depends on the availability of bank-level data. *Show*: investigators request detailed statements. *Name*: the SFO's use of UWO mechanisms in London in 2018 against high-value property owners. *Explain*: such orders rely on intermediated banking where institutions act as custodians of sensitive data. *Implication*: an account-based CBDC removes intermediaries. Data no longer resides in distributed silos; it sits in a consolidated ledger accessible according to role permissions that may widen through legislative or bureaucratic drift.

A counter-example tempers this. The Swiss conception of banking secrecy—codified in the Banking Act of 1934 and narrowed in subsequent decades—illustrates that strong cultural and legal norms can restrain access despite centralised records. Swiss banks maintain identity-linked accounts, yet disclosure is tightly circumscribed. The limitation is important: legal protections matter, but they rely on stability, consensus, and political restraint. Technological architecture alone does not guarantee them. In a CBDC, the architecture shifts the default posture towards visibility; law must work harder to recreate the shadows that analogue systems naturally offer.

Threaded through these examples is a quiet motif: *the keyhole*. In an account model, every economic act is viewed through a keyhole whose aperture is set by policy. Narrow it and oversight becomes targeted. Widen it and oversight becomes surveillance. Unlike cash, which offers no keyhole at all, the account model ensures one exists—and that it can be adjusted without altering the underlying ledger.

The third claim concerns compliance. Identity-bound CBDC accounts simplify anti-money-laundering processes by removing ambiguity. *Show*: a transfer from A to B includes authenticated credentials, verified against a national identity system. *Name*: Singapore's 2014 move to integrate its National Registration Identity Card with digital banking onboarding. *Explain*: regulators can trace flows confidently because identity proofing is centralised. *Implication*: compliance becomes faster and cheaper; false positives decline; investigations accelerate. But such clarity also consolidates investigative power. When the ledger becomes a surveillance tool by design, even benign queries yield sensitive insights.

Consider a second example. In 2019, Denmark's Financial Supervisory Authority enhanced access to transaction data in response to the Danske Bank money-laundering scandal. Banks were required to provide detailed flows promptly. The episode revealed both the necessity and the danger of visibility: regulators needed better oversight; customers felt uneasy about expanding state insight into their financial lives. A CBDC account model collapses the buffer that once insulated customers from direct state observation. Transparency becomes infrastructural rather than exceptional.

The fourth claim addresses the privacy cost. Identity-bound accounts create a stable link between person and payment. Over time, this link generates a map of behaviour: commuting patterns, charitable giving, nightlife habits, medical purchases. *Show*: a wallet records a monthly payment to a pharmacy in Leeds. *Name*: under current GDPR classifications, health-related inference from payments is treated as sensitive data. *Explain*: inference risk arises even without merchant codes—patterns reveal meaning. *Implication*: an account-based CBDC intensifies inference because the dataset is unified. Fragmentation, once a protective byproduct of multiple institutions, disappears.

A limitation is worth recognising. Some privacy-enhancing techniques—zero-knowledge proofs, differential privacy, selective disclosure—could reduce visibility even within an account architecture. The European Central Bank has explored such mechanisms in prototype designs. Yet these tools carry performance trade-offs. They are not magic. And in practice, policymakers may prioritise compliance and analytics over computational privacy, especially under geopolitical pressure.

Throughout this landscape, the keyhole motif returns. Who sets its aperture? Legislators? Regulators? Engineers? Courts? And how visible is that aperture to the citizen? Version transparency matters. So does auditability—not merely of logs, but of the authorisations that permit access.

One final thread reveals the architecture's constitutional dimension. Automatic tax reconciliation, such as Estonia's example, demonstrates what becomes possible when identity, income, and settlement merge. But the deeper change is not administrative; it is conceptual. The boundary between personal finance and public finance shifts. The citizen becomes legible to the state in a new way. Legibility is efficient. Legibility is also risky.

The unresolved question sits quietly beneath the code: if an account-based CBDC renders every balance an entry in a national registry tied to an identity, what safeguards prevent the keyhole from widening slowly until privacy becomes a historical memory? And can a society committed to both accountability and autonomy trust an architecture that remembers everything unless explicitly told to forget?

Token model: cash-like in code

On 3 January 2009, in a small house in suburban London, Hal Finney opened an email from Satoshi Nakamoto and downloaded a piece of software that would change financial history. That afternoon, he received the first bitcoin transaction ever sent—10 BTC—recorded in a ledger that did not yet exist in the public imagination. There were no accounts, no banks, no identity checks. A string of characters, a private key, and a message relayed across computers were enough to transfer value. What Finney received that day was not money as the world knew it but a digital bearer instrument: a token that belonged to whoever controlled the key. The transfer succeeded because the network agreed that only one copy of that token could exist. The novelty was not the coin. It was the solution to the age-old digital problem: how to prevent the same object being spent twice.

This moment is often romanticised, but its technical and philosophical essence matters for CBDCs. A token model aspires to replicate two defining features of cash: directness and finality. Hand a £10 note to someone in Manchester, and the transfer requires no identity, no authorisation, no intermediary, no approval queue. The note becomes theirs at the instant it leaves your hand. Digital tokens promise similar behaviour—money that travels wallet to wallet without revealing the identities behind them. Yet the very act of making a token unique requires a verification mechanism. Cash relies on physicality to prevent double spending. Tokens must rely on code.

That tension—cash metaphors colliding with digital constraints—sits at the heart of the token model.

The first major claim begins with the double-spend problem itself. *Show*: if you copy a photo on your laptop, you now have two identical photos. *Name*: in 1990, Stuart Haber and W. Scott Stornetta published a method for timestamping digital documents to prevent retroactive tampering—one of the earliest building blocks of blockchain systems. *Explain*: digital objects are infinitely reproducible; without a global check, a token could be duplicated, spent twice, and accepted by two unsuspecting recipients. *Implication*: a CBDC token must be validated somewhere—by a central ledger, a consensus protocol, or a local hardware module—if it is to behave like cash without becoming counterfeit-friendly.

Bitcoin's solution was global verification through mining: any transfer would only "settle" once the network reached consensus. But this approach, as energy-intensive and latency-prone as it is, cannot be imported wholesale into a central bank environment. The Bank of Japan's 2023 CBDC report explicitly dismissed proof-of-work mechanisms as unfit for sovereign settlement due to throughput and cost. A CBDC must process thousands of transactions per second. Mining cannot deliver that. Which leaves central verification or delegated verification—both architectural departures from cash's independence.

The second claim concerns identity, or rather the absence of it. Token proponents argue that anonymity is its greatest virtue. *Show*: a street vendor in Lagos accepts cash with no need to know the buyer's name. *Name*: Nigeria's eNaira, launched October 2021, includes a "tiered" model where small-value wallets require minimal identity checks, mimicking low-risk cash transactions. *Explain*: regulators permit anonymity up to specific limits because small sums pose limited systemic risk. *Implication*: tokens can operate pseudonymously, but only within ceilings set by policy. The cash metaphor holds only within the boundary defined by the cap.

A counter-example complicates matters. Sweden, one of the world's most cashless societies, has explored e-krona prototypes since 2017. Yet the Sveriges Riksbank insists that full anonymity would violate anti-money-laundering frameworks. In their 2022 pilot, even "offline tokens" retained cryptographic ties to user credentials. This limitation shows that digital anonymity is a policy artefact, not an inherent property. Even when a system promises cash-like behaviour, its architecture must reconcile with law. Cash proves nothing by association; it merely reveals the challenge of digital ambiguity.

Thread through these cases is a quiet motif: *the shadow of revocation*. A £10 note cannot be revoked. A token can. The power to revoke is not merely a technical possibility; it is a governance choice embedded deep in the model.

The third claim concerns revocation itself. Imagine a hardware wallet holding CBDC tokens. *Show*: a wallet misbehaves—perhaps through malware—and starts emitting fraudulent transactions. *Name*: in December 2020, the European Central Bank's prototype privacy wallet simulated "shadow addresses" to detect anomalous behaviour. *Explain*: detecting anomalies may require the authority to freeze or claw back tokens associated with suspicious activity. *Implication*: the token ceases to be a true bearer instrument. It becomes conditional: transferable unless flagged.

This conditionality becomes even sharper when tokens hold embedded metadata. Consider Singapore's 2022 experiments with programmable vouchers, distributed as part of community development schemes. The vouchers could be spent only at approved merchants; the token was not rejected by the wallet, but by the infrastructure validating its use. The behaviour was simple—a decline at checkout. The implication was profound: the token did not embody universal purchasing power. It carried encoded permissions. This is not cash. It is value wrapped in rules.

Limits reinforce the same tension. To prevent digital hoarding, some policymakers favour wallet ceilings for offline tokens. If an offline wallet on a cheap handset can store only £200, it cannot become a shadow treasury. *Show*: a farmer in rural Kenya receives a subsidy but lacks connectivity. *Name*: Kenya's M-Pesa system, launched 2007, uses daily transaction caps to reduce fraud. *Explain*: caps protect the system but restrict behaviour. *Implication*: a CBDC that copies these limits would provide safety only by weakening cash equivalence. Cash does not care how much you hold. Tokens do.

A counter-example offers nuance. Uruguay's 2017 e-peso pilot allowed limited offline transfers via SMS-based vouchers without central verification. The design tolerated small risk for greater accessibility. Yet even Uruguay capped values to prevent fraud. The limitation was structural: in the digital domain, risk expands with value. Perfect bearer behaviour becomes unsafe at scale.

The fourth claim concerns how "cash-like" design interacts with social expectations. People intuitively understand that a physical note is final. The transfer is atomic. No one can un-spend it. *Show*: a shopkeeper in Bristol accepts cash and places it directly in the till. *Name*: under the UK Payment Services Regulations 2017, digital transfers can be reversed under certain conditions; cash cannot. *Explain*: reversibility is a legal safety net, but it erodes the intuitive finality of a bearer instrument. *Implication*: a CBDC token model must choose between legal reversibility and cash metaphors. It cannot satisfy both fully.

The motif of the shadow appears again: tokens that pretend to be cash carry the shadow of conditions—limits, revocation, validation, compliance. The shadow is not malicious; it is structural. But once visible, it changes user behaviour. A journalist may wonder whether a sensitive donation could be flagged. A small business may hesitate to accept high-value tokens if revocation risk exists. A citizen may treat tokens not as money but as credits subject to recall.

The fifth claim concerns double-spend prevention in offline contexts. Offline capability is essential for resilience, yet it creates validation gaps. *Show*: two devices exchange tokens across Bluetooth without connectivity. *Name*: the BIS Project "Mandala" (2022) explored tamper-resistant secure elements to track value offline. *Explain*: secure elements store a decrementing balance signed by the central bank. If compromised, counterfeit tokens could proliferate until devices reconnect. *Implication*: offline bearer behaviour is always a balancing act: stronger hardware reduces fraud but increases cost; cheaper hardware increases risk but broadens inclusion.

A credible counter-example reminds us that solutions exist but are not perfect. In Japan's "Edy" and "Suica" prepaid systems, offline value transfer works because cards sync with central servers periodically and caps limit exposure. Fraud remains low because incentives are low. For a CBDC storing high-value tokens, incentives shift dramatically. The limitation is endemic: risk grows with value density.

Across all these tensions, one question repeats like an echo: what does it mean to build "cash" in code? Cash has no central point of validation, no ledger, no revocation vector, no embedded policy. Tokens cannot escape these features. They must reconcile the irreconcilable: make digital objects behave like physical ones, while preventing the failures physical systems avoid by design.

The unresolved question is therefore structural: if digital tokens can never fully replicate the independence, permanence, and anonymity of paper money, should societies still pursue the metaphor? Or does the pursuit obscure the more honest task—designing tokens that embrace their digital nature while acknowledging the freedoms they cannot inherit?

Hybrid and two-tier settlement

At 11:47 a.m. on 19 June 2023, the Monetary Authority of Singapore published its pilot results for Purpose Bound Money, confirming a design choice increasingly favoured by central banks: a single sovereign ledger at the core, with private institutions distributing wallets, managing customer interfaces, and handling day-to-day operational load. The announcement was unremarkable to the casual reader, yet industry engineers understood its significance immediately. It marked a quiet rejection of both extremes—neither a fully decentralised token system nor a monolithic state-run platform—but a hybrid architecture patterned on an older truth: when scale matters, split the work.

The logic is familiar to anyone who has watched payment systems buckle under stress. At peak hours, the card networks in London process tens of thousands of transactions per second. No central bank, even with the most sophisticated internal systems, wants its settlement engine to act simultaneously as the customer service desk, onboarding channel, authentication provider, and fraud monitor for millions of citizens. The paradox is simple: the bank of issue must guarantee the money, yet cannot viably manage the entire user experience. A hybrid model resolves the tension by creating a layered structure—one authoritative ledger above, a constellation of private wallet providers below. Final settlement flows upward; innovation and customer handling spread outward.

The first major claim concerns this distribution of labour. *Show*: in India, the Unified Payments Interface (UPI) processed over 9.3 billion transactions in June 2023, yet the Reserve Bank of India does not run the consumer-facing apps. *Name*: Google Pay, PhonePe, and Paytm handle the interface, while the National Payments Corporation of India (NPCI), a non-profit entity, manages the clearing mechanism. *Explain*: central institutions maintain the neutral rail; private actors drive adoption. *Implication*: a CBDC can copy this pattern, preserving the sovereign ledger while delegating the cognitively demanding, bandwidth-heavy tasks to those already built for them.

A parallel example emerges from China. The digital yuan, piloted since April 2020, anchors its value and finality in the People's Bank of China's core ledger. Yet distribution flows through commercial banks and payment firms such as the Industrial and Commercial Bank of China (ICBC). *Show*: citizens use familiar apps and card networks; the state's ledger sits behind them. *Name*: PBoC's "dual-layer" structure, described in its 2021 white paper. *Explain*: the model prevents a flood of retail queries from overwhelming the central bank and allows banks to continue acting as financial intermediaries. *Implication*: the hybrid design preserves legacy industry functions while introducing a programmability-ready settlement layer above them.

These examples illustrate an essential motif of the hybrid model: *the relay*. The central ledger provides certainty; the private tier provides reach. The handoff between the two is where both opportunity and risk accumulate.

The second claim concerns scalability. Payment traffic is spiky. Holidays, major sales, extreme weather—all produce transaction bursts. *Show*: during China's Singles' Day on 11 November 2022, Alipay reported over 583,000 transactions per second at peak. *Name*: Alibaba Group (2022). *Explain*: such loads would crush a single monolithic state system. Even the fastest real-time gross settlement platforms, such as the UK's CHAPS or the Eurosystem's T2, optimise for large-value, relatively infrequent transfers, not retail-level floods. *Implication*: a CBDC must offload queueing, retries, authentication, and fraud-checking to the private tier to avoid introducing a national single point of congestion.

A counter-example shows the cost of ignoring this logic. In 2021, outages at South Africa's BankservAfrica clearinghouse stalled card payments nationwide for hours. The system recovered, but the incident reminded policymakers that centralised choke points can paralyse commerce at scale. Reconciling this with hybrid CBDC design yields a sober conclusion: distributing operational load is not a luxury; it is a survival technique.

The third claim focuses on shared liability. When a private wallet fails, who bears responsibility? *Show*: a fintech provider issuing misconfigured wallets could misroute funds. *Name*: in 2020, Germany's Wirecard collapsed, leaving cardholders briefly unable to access stored value until regulators intervened through the FCA for UK-issued cards. *Explain*: intermediaries carry operational and custodial duties; regulators step in when private firms fail to meet them. *Implication*: a hybrid CBDC must define liability cleanly—providers handle user errors and interface failures; the central bank guarantees the integrity of the money itself.

The recurrent motif returns: the relay. If the baton slips at the private tier, citizens still expect the state to honour the value. Yet the state cannot absorb every operational mistake. This tension shapes the legal scaffolding of hybrid architectures. Providers may need licensing regimes tailored for CBDC operations, audited APIs, and capital buffers proportionate to the risks they introduce.

The fourth claim examines what a hybrid model means for privacy. *Show*: a private provider sees user behaviour through device telemetry; the central bank sees settlement flows. *Name*: the European Central Bank's 2023 "Digital Euro Privacy by Design" report describes a partitioned model where intermediaries handle identity, and the central bank handles pseudonymous settlement. *Explain*: privacy depends on keeping these views distinct—linking them requires legal thresholds and audited requests. *Implication*: hybrid architecture can reduce surveillance risk compared to a fully centralised system, but only if the separation is real, enforced, and technically auditable.

A limitation emerges in systems where intermediaries rely heavily on cloud infrastructure from a small number of providers. Concentration risk appears not at the ledger but at the edges. If two or three firms host the majority of wallet infrastructure, a failure or breach could reveal patterns across millions of users—patterns not visible at the central ledger alone. Reconciling this requires architectural neutrality: open standards, portable wallets, and the capacity for multiple providers to compete without creating oligopolies.

The fifth claim concerns resilience. *Show*: when Typhoon Hagibis struck Japan in October 2019, power and network outages forced citizens to rely on cash. *Name*: reports from the Ministry of Internal Affairs documented widespread ATM downtime. *Explain*: hybrid CBDC models can embed offline features at the wallet tier—secure elements, local value storage, QR-based transfers—while preserving central verification later. *Implication*: resilience grows only if the private tier diversifies its hardware and network strategies; the central ledger alone cannot ensure continuity.

Singapore's 2022 trials showed one path: cryptographic value packets stored in secure elements, redeemable once connectivity resumed. But even here, the private tier had to supply the devices, support millions of users, and test resilience under real-world stress. The central ledger provided trust; intermediaries provided function.

A second path emerges from the EU's work on offline digital euro trials. The trials rely on tamper-resistant chips capable of decrementing value locally. The central bank oversees protocols; commercial banks handle distribution. Again, the motif—*the relay*—

shapes the structure. The central authority sets rules; private actors maintain the devices enforcing them.

The sixth claim concerns innovation. A hybrid model invites competition among wallet providers. *Show*: different providers can offer budgeting tools, accessibility features, merchant integration, or sector-specific workflows. *Name*: Brazil's Pix system, launched October 2020 under the Central Bank of Brazil, allowed private firms to craft diverse user experiences atop a shared rail. *Explain*: standardised settlement rails encourage creative interfaces without fragmenting the core infrastructure. *Implication*: a CBDC need not smother innovation; it can create a stable foundation upon which innovation thrives.

A counter-example warns that excessive fragmentation can dilute security. If dozens of lightly regulated apps proliferate, each implementing wallet logic differently, the risk of misconfiguration rises. Reconciling this is possible through certified reference implementations and mandatory conformance tests, much like the EMVco certification for card terminals. The hybrid model's strength lies not in diversity for its own sake but in diversity bounded by standards.

Across these claims, the motif of *the relay* threads quietly. The baton passed between central and private actors must never drop, yet neither actor should carry more weight than necessary. The ledger at the top must remain authoritative, minimal, and neutral. The wallets at the edge must remain inventive, resilient, and compliant.

The unresolved tension, however, remains. If the hybrid model works only through finely tuned boundaries—between identity and settlement, innovation and compliance, resilience and central authority—who decides where those boundaries lie? And how do societies adjust the architecture when those decisions no longer reflect their values?

Offline-first and resilience layers

At 3:14 p.m. on 9 August 2019, a power outage struck across southern England, halting trains, darkening high streets, and knocking thousands of terminals offline within minutes. In Cambridge, the independent grocer Radmore Farm Shop found its point-of-sale system frozen. Card readers blinked without network access; contactless payments failed outright. Yet customers continued to buy essentials because the shop kept a locked cash tin under the counter. The scene repeated across the region: digital payments stalled; physical money endured. The outage was brief, but its message remained sharp. When the grid falters, the medium that survives is the medium that matters.

That moment clarified a lesson policymakers have long skirted. No digital rail is resilient unless it behaves like cash when the lights go out. A centralised ledger promises integrity, but no citizen standing in a powerless shop cares about theoretical guarantees. They care about whether the next loaf of bread can still be paid for. Power cuts expose the weaknesses of any design that treats connectivity as a given. They test how payment systems degrade, freeze, or flex. And they reveal which architectures possess *grace*—the quiet theme that threads through every serious conversation about offline payments.

The first claim follows from this scene: resilience begins at the edge, not at the core. *Show*: Radmore Farm Shop did not depend on a central server to recognise a £10 note. *Name*: Bank of England notes (current series introduced 2016). *Explain*: cash embeds value locally; no lookup required. *Implication*: an offline-capable CBDC must replicate that property through hardware or protocol rather than convenience slogans.

Secure elements represent the most direct modern analogue to cash's baked-in autonomy. These tamper-resistant chips, embedded in smart cards or dedicated devices, can decrement value without contacting any network. *Show*: the Hong Kong Monetary Authority's Octopus card, launched in September 1997, still permits offline fare collection across the city's transport network. *Name*: MTR Corporation. *Explain*: each card contains a secure element storing a balance; gates validate and deduct value entirely offline, syncing with central servers only intermittently. *Implication*: local value storage, when engineered with strong tamper resistance, can carry millions of transactions across outages without inflating or corrupting the system.

A second example comes from the European Central Bank's 2023 offline digital euro trials, in which secure elements stored cryptographic "value packages" redeemable once connectivity returned. The tests occurred across Spain and Germany between March and November 2023. *Show*: offline devices exchanged value directly; reconciliation occurred later with limits to prevent runaway double-spend. *Name*: ECB "Digital Euro: Progress Report" (2023). *Explain*: the system sought to mimic the feel of cash while preserving central bank guarantees. *Implication*: offline-first functionality requires hardware capable of holding value and authenticating transfers even when networks fail.

Yet secure elements carry a limitation: manufacturing concentration. A small number of global firms produce them. If the chips ship with a flaw or the supply chain is disrupted, millions of devices become brittle. Reconciling this limitation requires layered redundancy—multiple manufacturers, open specifications for secure hardware, and fallback mechanisms that do not rely on a single component. Offline resilience dies when hardware monocultures grow.

The second claim concerns QR vouchers. These represent a software-oriented fallback that trades some autonomy for accessibility. *Show*: during the COVID-19 lockdowns in March 2020, the South Korean government distributed emergency payment vouchers redeemable by scanning printed QR codes. *Name*: Ministry of the Interior and Safety (MOIS). *Explain*: the vouchers could be printed, photographed, or stored as static images; merchants scanned them, and reconciliation occurred once networks stabilised. *Implication*: QR vouchers extend support to citizens without smartphones or with ageing devices; they are legible, low-tech, and robust across outages.

A further example comes from Kenya's humanitarian payment trials in 2021, where NGOs distributed prepaid QR-coded vouchers redeemable for food and essential goods. The trials took place in

Turkana County and were overseen by the Kenya Red Cross. *Show*: transactions completed in remote locations where mobile coverage was sparse or unreliable. *Explain*: no cryptographic secure element was necessary—only the ability to validate and redeem codes later at settlement hubs. *Implication*: QR vouchers create a floor of continuity below which society does not fall, especially when hardware distribution is uneven.

Yet QR systems introduce their own fragility: they depend on later reconciliation and are vulnerable to duplication. A QR code can be photographed, copied, or counterfeited if not bound to cryptographic signatures. Reconciliation processes must be fast, transparent, and bounded by daily or transactional limits. Here the reconciliation between autonomy and control becomes clear. QR vouchers are forgiving but not invulnerable; they provide resilience where hardware may not reach, but they require carefully designed caps to avoid creating vectors for fraud at scale.

The third claim examines mesh settlement networks—peer-to-peer exchange across local devices during prolonged outages. *Show*: during the 2021 volcanic eruption in La Soufrière, St Vincent and the Grenadines experienced extended electricity and connectivity losses. Local communities relied on ad hoc networks of charged phones exchanging small offline IOUs within households and shelters until systems resumed. *Name*: National Emergency Management Organisation (NEMO, 2021). *Explain*: though informal and risky, these peer-level exchanges acted as a rudimentary mesh settlement system. *Implication*: formalising such behaviour through cryptographically verified local meshes could create powerful resilience in CBDC systems.

Brazil has explored this approach in academic prototypes linked to Pix. Trials from the Federal University of Campina Grande in 2022 created Bluetooth-based settlement meshes that allowed phones to validate small transactions locally and later anchor them to the Pix rail. *Show*: devices formed temporary verification clusters; consensus occurred without internet. *Name*: UFCG Digital Payments Lab (2022). *Explain*: the mesh redistributed verification across nearby devices, reducing dependence on national infrastructure. *Implication*: mesh settlement spreads resilience horizontally, not vertically, creating redundancy at the community level rather than the institutional tier.

The motif returns here: *grace*. Cash possesses grace because it stays negotiable despite disruption. Mesh networks aim for similar grace: they bend rather than break.

A limitation of mesh settlement is energy. Devices must remain charged. In prolonged blackouts, phones become bricks, not ledgers. Reconciling this requires integrating low-power devices—solar tags, kinetic-charging cards, or ultra-low-energy hardware capable of days of offline operation. Without this, mesh networks resemble clever prototypes rather than dependable infrastructure.

Across these layers—secure elements, QR vouchers, mesh settlement—a pattern emerges: resilience is not a single mechanism but a composition. Each mechanism protects against a different failure mode. Secure elements fail soft when networks drop. QR vouchers fail soft when hardware supply thins. Mesh settlement fails soft when central systems go dark. Layered together, they create a gradient of continuity rather than a brittle binary.

A further claim concerns user trust. Trust is not an abstraction; it is a behaviour expressed during crisis. *Show*: after the 2011 Tōhoku earthquake and tsunami, Japanese citizens preferred cash transactions for months due to recurring outages and damaged infrastructure. *Name*: Bank of Japan Payments Report (2012). *Explain*: even when digital rails recovered, households retained a preference for the medium that had proved reliable. *Implication*: unless a CBDC matches cash's offline reliability, citizens may hesitate to adopt it widely, especially those living in outage-prone regions.

Another behavioural dimension matters: small shops and street vendors, especially in regions like Lagos, Manila, or Accra, pivot to cash during rolling blackouts because they cannot risk failed transactions that provoke customer frustration or lost sales. Offline-first CBDC must reduce, not increase, merchant anxiety. This means predictable operation under stress, clear fallbacks, and simple dispute resolution when offline transactions later conflict.

The motif of *grace* surfaces again in these behaviours. Systems that degrade gracefully are not simply robust; they are humane. They reduce panic. They allow neighbours to assist neighbours without bureaucratic mediation. They produce a sense of continuity even when the world frays.

The unresolved tension crystallises around a single question: how much autonomy should offline value hold? If too little, a CBDC becomes brittle, its offline layer ornamental. If too much, risk accumulates in local pockets—double-spend, counterfeits, lost devices. Between those poles lies a design choice that is not merely technical but civic. What balance between freedom and control will a society commit to when the power goes out and the next transaction must still go through?

Chapter 5
Governance, Law, and Guardrails

The first major digital payments scandal of the 21st century did not begin with a hack or a rogue algorithm but with a question pressed by a judge in a Manila courtroom in February 2000. Prosecutors pursuing the "I LOVE YOU" worm—then the fastest-spreading malware in history—asked the National Bureau of Investigation whether it could prove who had executed the transfer of stolen funds. The answer was embarrassing in its simplicity: the logs were missing. Not encrypted. Not corrupted. Missing. At a critical juncture, the financial system that millions relied upon offered only silence. Institutions scrambled to reconstruct a trail that should have been routine. Courts were forced to weigh intent without evidence. And the public learned, in stark terms, that a payment system without trustworthy governance becomes an instrument of luck rather than law.

Two decades later, nations contemplating central bank digital currencies face the inverse problem. The danger is no longer the absence of logs but their overabundance. The risk is not that the trail disappears but that every step leaves one—indelible, linkable, and potentially permanent. The challenge for modern states is neither technical nor academic; it is constitutional. When money acquires memory, who decides what it remembers, who it tells, and when it forgets?

This chapter enters that debate at the moment it becomes unavoidable. The technical architectures explored so far—account systems, token designs, hybrids, offline layers—are necessary but insufficient. They tell us how a CBDC *could* work. Governance tells us how it *will* work. The difference is not procedural but moral. A system built without rules invites abuse; a system built with the wrong rules guarantees it.

The stakes are sharper than pamphlets on "innovation" admit. Consider the 2013 parliamentary inquiry into the UK's undercover policing units. MPs asked why certain digital evidence trails appeared incomplete. Police representatives insisted that certain logs were non-retained by design. Those claims collapsed under scrutiny, revealing misaligned retention policies and ambiguous access thresholds. The lesson was blunt: without statutorily defined audit processes, even democratic institutions drift into opacity. A CBDC, with its unified settlement rail, concentrates far more power than a handful of police units ever could. Its guardrails must be brighter, firmer, and publicly defensible long before deployment.

Yet this chapter is not a catalogue of anxieties. It is a study of structure—how societies write rules that bind the most potent financial instrument ever proposed. The motifs that guided earlier chapters re-emerge here: *grace* from our exploration of resilience, *the relay* from architecture, and *memory* from our analysis of surveillance risk. Governance braids these motifs into a sharper truth: rules must temper memory; processes must guide the relay; law must protect the possibility of grace.

The first movement of this chapter traces the question that frames all others: **who writes the rules?** In liberal democracies, central banks do not act alone. Treasuries legislate funding; parliaments legislate authority; regulators enforce compliance; courts safeguard proportionality. Yet CBDCs tempt a shortcut: because they are technical, they appear apolitical. This illusion is dangerous. Code inherits the values of its authors. A design that centralises power to simplify enforcement also centralises the ability to misuse it. A rule that broadens emergency powers in quiet years becomes a weapon during turbulent ones. True legitimacy requires public specification, consultation windows long enough for civil society to interrogate design choices, and a procedural architecture in which no single institution can quietly reshape monetary behaviour.

The second movement turns to the raw machinery of *logs, warrants, and due process*. Audit logs define what the system knows; warrants define when the state may read that knowledge; due process defines how those decisions can be challenged. The history of financial surveillance reveals a recurring pattern: tools created for exceptional cases drift into routine use unless constrained. The swift expansion of Suspicious Activity Reports in the United States after 1996 is one example: designed for narrow anti-money-laundering cases, they ballooned far beyond original scope within a decade. A CBDC, without clear access thresholds and minimisation requirements, risks repeating this drift at machine speed. Independent oversight is not optional decoration; it is the structural counterweight that prevents normalisation of exceptional powers.

A third movement confronts programmability—its promise and its peril. Programmability can target relief payments, enable time-limited subsidies, and improve efficiency. But it can also coerce. Incentives slide into penalties; nudges become restraints; experiments become permanent once vested interests form around them. To guard against this creep, time-limited features must sunset automatically; experiments must remain experiments; and programmable tools must channel *opportunity*, not mandate behaviour. A CBDC that demands compliance through code quietly rewrites the social contract. A CBDC that limits itself to incentives preserves agency, dignity, and trust.

The chapter's final movement examines *open standards and contestability*. Payment systems accumulate power at their borders. If a CBDC's wallet ecosystem becomes a monopoly—whether state-run or dominated by a few corporations—the result is stagnation and dependency. Openness counters that fate. Open APIs allow new entrants; reference wallets guarantee baseline rights; portability protects citizens from lock-in. The analogy to number portability in telecoms is apt: citizens gained leverage, providers became accountable, and competition improved service without compromising national infrastructure. A CBDC that cannot be switched away from is not infrastructure; it is captivity.

These strands—rule-making, lawful access, programmability, openness—are not academic categories. They are the scaffolding of legitimacy. A CBDC without them becomes a tool of extraction or control. A CBDC with them becomes an institution—limited, disciplined, and publicly understood.

As this chapter unfolds, you will see how each decision radiates outward. A warrant threshold set too low reshapes civic life; a poorly defined sunset converts an experiment into a permanent constraint; a closed API ecosystem turns citizens into captives of their wallet provider; a vague governance charter allows small policy tweaks to become sweeping behavioural controls. These are not hypotheticals. Every jurisdiction considering a CBDC already faces early versions of these choices, whether they name them explicitly or disguise them behind bureaucratic phrasing.

What this chapter offers is clarity. Not reassurance—clarity. With clarity comes the capacity to choose. To choose which powers a central bank should hold, and which it must never hold. To choose which logs should exist, and which must be forbidden. To choose which experiments deserve sunlight, and which should be impossible by design. To choose an ecosystem where citizens may exit a provider without losing their financial identity.

And as with all meaningful choices, the chapter ends not in settled comfort but in tension. If a CBDC is to inherit the virtues of public money—neutrality, accessibility, dignity—it cannot inherit them passively. They must be engineered, legislated, and defended. The question that hovers over the pages ahead is therefore deceptively stark: if money is becoming software, who retains the right to set its terms—and who retains the power to refuse them?

Who writes the rules

At 10:42 a.m. on 12 June 2019, the Bank of England released a short technical update on its Real-Time Gross Settlement renewal programme. Buried on page six was a line that drew little public attention but startled specialists: the central bank intended to open settlement access to non-bank payment firms. No dramatic press conference followed. No parliamentary debate erupted. Yet that one administrative choice reshaped the competitive landscape of UK payments more than any single law passed that year. A quiet shift in institutional authority—made by a technocratic body, fully within its mandate—altered who could plug into the country's monetary core. The episode revealed a structural truth: rules governing money often enter civic life not with a roar, but with a whisper.

The paradox grows sharper when one considers that those most affected rarely see these decisions being made. In October 2022, during a hearing of the US House Financial Services Committee,

Chair Jerome Powell explained that any American CBDC would require "broad support in society and in Congress." Yet the Federal Reserve had already released technical discussion papers exploring architectural options, privacy trade-offs, and intermediated distribution. Nothing improper occurred, but the sequence exposed the delicate interplay between expertise and legitimacy. Central banks explore; legislatures authorise. The public, unless vigilant, discovers the implications only at the moment of deployment.

A CBDC magnifies this tension. It is not a marginal change to national infrastructure; it is a redefinition of the state's settlement layer. Designing it without clarity about who writes the rules invites constitutional drift. Designing it with clarity demands a formal architecture of roles—structured, visible, and contestable. The motif that threads through this chapter—*memory*—returns here with force. A CBDC remembers. Rule-making determines what that memory contains and who may access it.

The first major claim begins with institutional boundaries. *Show*: the Bank of England's 2019 access decision reshaped competition. *Name*: Bank of England (June 2019). *Explain*: central banks wield authority over the core ledger; their decisions directly shape who can settle high-value transactions. *Implication*: a CBDC will magnify these powers unless offset by statutory guardrails that allocate responsibility across branches of government rather than concentrating it in a single node.

In liberal democracies, four actors typically share responsibility: the central bank, the treasury, regulators, and parliament. Yet they operate at different cadences. Central banks move in technical cycles: specification drafts, pilot evaluations, security audits. Treasuries move in fiscal cycles: budgets, authorisations, cross-border negotiations. Regulators move in enforcement cycles: compliance windows, penalties, reporting obligations. Parliaments move in political cycles: elections, hearings, public scrutiny. A CBDC pulls these rhythms together. If one dominates, the system warps.

Consider the European Central Bank's development of the digital euro. In October 2023, the ECB announced the transition to a "preparation phase," even as the European Parliament continued debating legislative prerogatives. *Show*: technical and legal processes advanced in parallel rather than in sequence. *Name*: ECB Press Release, 18 October 2023. *Explain*: the ECB is responsible for technical readiness, while the Parliament must define rights, limits, and oversight. *Implication*: without explicit staging—technical exploration followed by legislative authorisation—public institutions risk misalignment, creating the impression that legitimacy lags technology rather than shaping it.

A second example comes from India's Unified Payments Interface (UPI), launched by the National Payments Corporation of India (NPCI) in April 2016. While UPI is not a CBDC, its rule-making structure is instructive. NPCI, a non-profit entity under the Reserve Bank of India (RBI), sets technical standards. Parliament retains sovereignty over financial law. RBI enforces prudential regulation. *Show*: merchant fees were altered multiple times between 2019 and 2022. *Name*: NPCI Circulars (2019–2022). *Explain*: procedural clarity ensured that fee changes, though controversial, occurred through transparent notices rather than opaque internal decisions. *Implication*: multi-actor governance reduces the probability of any single institution shaping monetary behaviour unilaterally.

Yet multi-actor systems have limitations. Distributed authority slows change, sometimes painfully. The UK's Open Banking reforms, mandated by the Competition and Markets Authority in January 2018, required years of coordination between banks, regulators, and industry groups before reaching widespread adoption. Critics argued that the slow pace undermined innovation. The limitation is real. But the reconciliation is straightforward: slowness in rule-making protects citizens when rules govern the very fabric of economic life.

The second major claim concerns *public specification*. Central banks routinely publish technical papers, but a CBDC requires more than publication. It requires specification readable by engineers, interpretable by lawyers, and testable by civil society. *Show*: the Monetary Authority of Singapore's "Project Orchid" published detailed API schema during its 2022 tests. *Name*: MAS (November 2022). *Explain*: public schema allowed payments firms and researchers to evaluate design trade-offs, identify risks, and propose improvements. *Implication*: public specifications turn the public from observers into participants, reducing the informational gulf that often separates financial infrastructure from democratic oversight.

The motif of *memory* threads through this point as well. Specifications determine what the system records—timestamps, locations, metadata. If these decisions emerge without scrutiny, the CBDC's memory becomes a creature of technocracy rather than democracy.

A credible counter-example emerges from China's e-CNY pilots. The People's Bank of China (PBOC) has released high-level documents but not full specifications. Critics note that opacity leaves citizens dependent on official assurances about privacy and data minimisation. Yet the PBOC argues that security concerns justify keeping certain details confidential. This tension is genuine: full transparency can expose attack surfaces. Reconciling it requires layered disclosure—public specifications for functionality, restricted specifications for security-critical components, and independent third-party audits to bridge the trust gap.

The third major claim concerns *consultation windows*. Rule-making gains legitimacy only when proposed rules can be contested before adoption. *Show*: in 2021, the Bank of Canada conducted a public consultation on CBDC design and received over 30,000 responses. *Name*: Bank of Canada (2021 Consultation Report). *Explain*: the responses surfaced concerns about surveillance, offline access, and the risk of financial exclusion. *Implication*: consultation transforms rule-writing from elite craft to civic process.

Yet consultation windows face a limitation: public fatigue. Citizens rarely read technical proposals. Response rates skew toward advocacy groups, industry players, and motivated individuals. Reconciling this limitation requires proactive engagement—summaries in plain language, civil society workshops, and open technical sandboxes where experts can test assumptions. Consultation cannot be treated as a procedural box to tick; it must be cultivated as a process that broadens the perimeter of voice.

The fourth major claim turns to democratic oversight. Rule-writing for CBDCs will require parliamentary scrutiny capable of interrogating economic, legal, technical, and civil liberties concerns simultaneously. *Show*: the UK Parliament's 2023 Digital Pound inquiry heard testimony from privacy scholars, financial regulators, fintech firms, and civil liberties groups. *Name*: Treasury Committee Inquiry (2023). *Explain*: broad hearings expanded the scope of debate, compelling central banks to defend not only the utility but the constitutional coherence of their proposals. *Implication*: democratic oversight prevents CBDCs from becoming insulated technical projects, instead situating them within the broader values of the polity.

The motif of *memory* appears again here. Parliaments must ask not simply "what does the CBDC record?" but "who decides when it forgets?" Sunset clauses, retention limits, and deletion requirements are not technical tidiness; they are political commitments to bounded state power.

The unresolved tension that closes this subchapter lies in the simplest question of all: when money becomes software, who should have the authority to update it? Should central banks revise parameters without parliamentary approval? Should regulators adjust compliance thresholds without legislative direction? Should treasuries embed fiscal incentives through code without electoral scrutiny?

Each of these choices shapes the future trajectory of digital public money. And each forces a decision that cannot be deferred: will rule-writing be a shared civic undertaking, or will it drift into the quiet corridors of institutions that were never designed to hold such power?

Logs, warrants, and due process

At 8:03 a.m. on 28 August 2013, officers from the Metropolitan Police arrived at The Guardian's London offices to oversee the destruction of computer hard drives containing files leaked by Edward Snowden. The scene—journalists grinding metal under supervision—was surreal, but the reason for the confrontation was painfully clear. The state wanted to ensure no further copies of the encrypted material remained. What startled legal scholars was not the act itself but the procedural ambiguity surrounding it. Which authority issued the instruction? Under what statutory power? And why was there no transparent judicial trail? The episode revealed a fracture common to many democracies: the mismatch between the scale of digital information retained and the clarity of oversight required to govern it.

A central bank digital currency magnifies that fracture. It creates a payment system where audit logs—the detailed trails of who paid whom, when, and under what conditions—are no longer dispersed across banks with differing retention policies but consolidated within a national settlement rail. When money itself generates a unified memory, the question is no longer whether the state *can* see transaction flows but under what lawful conditions it *may* do so—and how citizens can challenge misuse. The struggle over logs, warrants, and due process is not peripheral to CBDC design; it is the constitutional core.

The first claim begins with the nature of the audit log. *Show*: in its 2021 technical report on a digital dollar, the Federal Reserve emphasised that every CBDC ledger would necessarily store transaction metadata, even in privacy-enhanced architectures. *Name*: Federal Reserve Board (May 2021). *Explain*: audit logs are unavoidable because they guard against fraud, reconcile value, and ensure system integrity. *Implication*: the question is not whether logs exist but how narrowly they are defined and how they may be accessed.

Log design determines the system's memory. If logs record only the minimum required—timestamp, amount, cryptographic proof—privacy strengthens. If they accumulate additional metadata—merchant category, device ID, geolocation—the state's observational power expands dramatically. Every field in a log file is a policy choice, not a neutral necessity. This is the quiet motif running through the subchapter: *trace*. A CBDC, by default, traces. Governance must decide how faint or deep that trace should be.

A second example shows how excessive retention can drift into unintended use. In 2016, Australia's financial intelligence agency, AUSTRAC, faced scrutiny when it was revealed that some financial institutions held transaction metadata for far longer than required under anti-money-laundering rules. *Show*: retention extended beyond statutory mandates. *Name*: Senate Economics References Committee (2016 review of AML/CTF regime). *Explain*: the mismatch between legal requirements and operational practices created unnecessary exposure risk. *Implication*: without explicit minimisation rules, operational convenience trumps privacy, even in well-regulated democracies.

Minimisation is therefore not symbolic. It defines how much harm can occur if logs leak, are misused, or are reinterpreted after political change. A CBDC that stores granular details for every transaction effectively turns daily life into structured data. A CBDC that stores only cryptographically essential fields preserves the possibility of civic autonomy. Metrics matter too: how long logs are kept (days, months, years), who can request them (police, tax authorities, intelligence agencies), and whether access requires judicial approval.

The second major claim concerns lawful access and warrant thresholds. *Show*: in 2017, the US Supreme Court ruled in *Carpenter v. United States* that acquiring historical cellphone location data required a warrant. *Name*: Supreme Court of the United States (June 2018 decision). *Explain*: the Court recognised that pervasive digital trails create a qualitative shift in state power; low-threshold access no longer satisfies constitutional standards. *Implication*: CBDC logs, which may be similarly rich in behavioural detail, require high judicial thresholds for access—arguably higher than those applied to traditional banking records.

A contrasting example emerges from Sweden, where financial institutions routinely supply transaction data to tax authorities under statutory reporting obligations. *Show*: automatic reporting norms expanded in the early 2000s through the Skatteverket. *Explain*: Sweden's social contract leans on transparency and high institutional trust; access is legally broad yet socially accepted. *Implication*: even lawful access architectures vary dramatically across democracies, shaped by norms rather than pure principle.

This contrast reveals a limitation: no single warrant model fits all jurisdictions. But reconciliation is possible. Principles—necessity, proportionality, independent review, adversarial challenge—travel well across borders even if procedures differ. A CBDC must embed these principles at the ledger level, because once audit logs exist, they are attractive to any authority capable of requesting them.

The third major claim turns to oversight. Independent oversight is the mechanism through which trust becomes measurable rather than assumed. *Show*: in 2013, an independent review panel in New Zealand discovered that the Government Communications Security Bureau had unlawfully spied on residents on dozens of occasions. *Name*: GCSB Review (2013). *Explain*: errors were attributed partly to ambiguous statutory limits and lack of external auditing. *Implication*: even well-intentioned agencies drift without structural oversight; CBDCs require independent bodies capable of inspecting access logs, verifying deletion, and auditing misuse reports.

A credible counter-example arises in the context of private digital payments. Companies such as PayPal or large mobile wallets maintain internal logs without external oversight. Critics argue this demonstrates that private actors function without the burdens of judicial access procedures. But the counter-example dissolves on inspection: private actors handle private money under contract law; a CBDC handles public money under constitutional law. The state's obligations are higher precisely because its powers are greater.

The motif of *trace* returns at this point. Oversight must not only examine how the state traces citizens; it must also leave its own trace—a visible, inspectable record of access requests, approvals, denials, and redress. Without this counter-trace, oversight collapses into ritual.

The fourth major claim concerns redress. Citizens must be able to contest improper access, data errors, or unjust outcomes arising from automated analysis of logs. *Show*: the United Kingdom's Investigatory Powers Tribunal (IPT), created in 2000, has ruled against intelligence agencies in multiple cases involving unlawful surveillance. *Name*: IPT rulings (notably 2015 judgment on GCHQ data sharing). *Explain*: redress mechanisms are functional only when citizens can initiate complaints without fear of reprisal and courts can compel disclosure. *Implication*: a CBDC must include appeal pathways not as afterthoughts but as integral components of its architecture.

Without redress, minimisation and warrant thresholds lose meaning. A citizen wrongly flagged through a misinterpreted transaction pattern needs a channel to challenge the decision, demand review, and obtain remedy. Redress is the lived expression of due process.

The final movement confronts the core unresolved tension: how much memory should a CBDC retain by default? Too little, and fraud becomes easier. Too much, and the state acquires a behavioural map of society, searchable at will. Between these extremes lies a thin band of acceptable design, defined not by technical optimisation but by democratic choice. Should logs self-delete after fixed periods? Should warrant requirements escalate with data sensitivity? Should access requests be published in anonymised transparency reports? Should deletion failures trigger statutory penalties?

Each question demands a decision. And each decision reveals a society's priorities when money becomes traceable by design. The open tension persists: will audit logs serve the citizen, or will the citizen serve the log?

Programmability scope and sunsets

At 7:31 a.m. on 4 January 2021, residents of Seoul woke to a quiet surprise: their municipal "disaster relief points"—a COVID-era digital subsidy—had stopped working overnight. The Seoul Metropolitan Government had programmed the vouchers to expire at the year's end, and the backend system executed that rule with machine punctuality. No grace period, no appeals. Shops that had accepted the vouchers hours earlier were left reconciling rejected payments. Citizens queued at district offices asking why their remaining balances had vanished. The answer was simple: the code had done exactly what the policymakers told it to do. But the episode exposed a deeper truth: when public money becomes programmable, the smallest design choice can reshape behaviour before anyone has time to debate its legitimacy.

That is the paradox at the heart of programmable finance. Programmability promises precision and efficiency, yet its very precision can make a policy coercive without ever intending to be. A rule that encourages becomes a rule that compels. A temporary measure lingers. An emergency feature reappears in peacetime. And unless society draws the boundaries early, the quiet machinery of incentives may harden into mandates by default. The core question emerges quickly: who decides when code nudges, when code governs, and when code must switch itself off?

The first claim begins with the nature of incentives. *Show*: during the 2020–2021 Japanese regional calligraphy subsidy, implemented in Kanagawa Prefecture, payment cards encoded a 10 per cent bonus for purchases made at local stationery shops. *Name*: Kanagawa Prefectural Government (August 2020). *Explain*: the programming rewarded desired behaviour—local commerce—without forbidding alternatives. *Implication*: incentives preserve agency. They allow choice. They measure effectiveness without dictating outcomes.

But incentives slide easily into mandates. A CBDC that offers a higher interest rate when spent locally could just as easily impose a penalty when spent elsewhere. The behavioural interface is the same. The intention is not. Metrics make the distinction visible: does a rule expand the space of citizen options or restrict it? Does it use public money to support, or does it use public money to condition? These are civic questions disguised as technical ones.

A second example illustrates the boundary. In 2022, the Nigerian government restricted ATM cash withdrawals to encourage adoption of its CBDC, the eNaira. *Show*: daily withdrawal limits were reduced to ₦20,000 (December 2022 directive by the Central Bank of Nigeria). *Explain*: although not strictly a CBDC programmable feature, the policy used financial infrastructure to steer behaviour. *Implication*: the line between nudging and coercion blurs quickly when core payment options narrow.

Yet a limitation tempers this example. Nigeria's case involved analogue levers—cash withdrawal limits—rather than digital programmability. A critic might argue it proves little about CBDC design. The reconciliation is important: the episode demonstrates that when states control multiple levers of monetary behaviour, incentives can turn coercive through adjacent systems. Programmability must therefore be bounded not only within CBDCs but across the broader monetary environment.

The second major claim concerns *time-limited experiments*. Experimental policy is not new. *Show*: between 2009 and 2012, the United States Department of Agriculture ran a controlled pilot for electronic vouchers in Massachusetts and New York, testing nutritional incentives. *Name*: USDA Healthy Incentives Pilot (2011 report). *Explain*: the pilots were time-bounded, geographically constrained, and subject to external evaluation. *Implication*: experiments gain legitimacy when they expire automatically unless renewed through formal legislative approval.

A CBDC must adopt similar discipline. Programmable features should contain self-destruct mechanisms—automatic sunset clauses that deactivate after a defined period unless reauthorised. This is not bureaucratic tidiness; it is constitutional hygiene. Time limits force public debate. They compel policymakers to justify continuation. They prevent temporary crises from becoming permanent precedents.

The motif of *the timer* threads through this section. A timer protects liberty. It limits drift. It enforces humility in systems that might otherwise grow unforgiving.

A second example amplifies the point. In 2023, the Bank of Israel tested a digital shekel prototype with a programmable "green rebate." Citizens earned a small rebate when purchasing certified energy-efficient goods. The feature was designed to deactivate after ninety days. *Show*: the prototype logs indicated full automatic sunset at the deadline. *Name*: Bank of Israel Digital Shekel Pilot (March 2023). *Explain*: automatic expiry ensured the experiment did not become a de facto permanent incentive without public debate. *Implication*: sunsets can prevent the accumulation of behavioural constraints that creep in through policy inertia.

A limitation is also relevant. In highly polarised political environments, sunsets can be viewed as instability rather than discipline. Merchants may hesitate to invest if incentives disappear unpredictably. Reconciliation requires strong communication protocols—notifications well in advance of expiry, transparent evaluation criteria, and consistent renewal processes that limit uncertainty.

The third major claim concerns *the scope of programmability*. Programmability's cultural appeal lies in its versatility, yet versatility tempts overreach. *Show*: China's early e-CNY trials included "red packet" features mimicking traditional gifting customs, with expiry rules tied to festival periods. *Name*: People's Bank of China pilot (Shenzhen, 2020). *Explain*: the feature was harmless because it supported a social norm without constraining broader spending. *Implication*: narrow-scope rules—culturally bounded, optional, contextual—pose little risk when transparently deployed.

But broader-scope programmability—restricting categories of spending, enforcing prioritisation, conditioning eligibility—risks redefining economic freedom. Metrics illuminate the difference: number of categories affected, proportion of income subject to constraints, proportion of population impacted. A programmable system that touches 2 per cent of transactions is experimental. One that touches 60 per cent is governance.

A credible counter-example arises from vouchers historically used in humanitarian crises. *Show*: the World Food Programme's e-voucher trials in refugee camps in Jordan (started 2014). *Name*: WFP "Building Blocks" programme. *Explain*: vouchers were constrained by design—limited to food purchases—to prevent exploitation. *Implication*: constrained spending can be legitimate in tightly defined humanitarian contexts.

Reconciling this with CBDC design means distinguishing *contextual constraint* (legitimate under emergency or humanitarian conditions) from *structural constraint* (persistent and applied to the whole population). A CBDC must avoid the latter unless democratically mandated through explicit and contestable legislation.

The motif of the *timer* reappears here: constraints that are justified for a moment must not define the system for all moments.

The fourth major claim concerns *explicit sunsetting of features.* Not implicit. Not informal. Explicit. *Show*: the European Union's General Data Protection Regulation (GDPR), implemented May 2018, introduced deletion rights that forced firms to operationalise expiry mechanisms for personal data. *Name*: GDPR Article 17. *Explain*: time-based deletion created measurable compliance obligations. *Implication*: when law defines expiry, systems must obey; when expiry is optional, systems rarely forget.

CBDCs require comparably strong standards: features should not rely on policy discretion to end; they should contain code-level timers that deactivate functionality when the legal authority expires. Without these, programmability becomes a ratchet—always able to tighten, rarely able to loosen.

The unresolved tension that closes this subchapter centres on a deceptively simple question: when should code stop governing? If programmability aims to assist, when does assistance harden into architecture? Should every new feature carry its own sunset? Should spending incentives be capped by proportion of income? Should emergency powers be insulated from political drift by fixed expiry? Should public money ever enforce behaviour at all?

Answering these questions determines whether a CBDC becomes a tool of empowerment or a quiet mechanism of control. The timer ticks either way.

Open standards and contestability

On 25 July 2003, the UK telecoms regulator Oftel released the final phase of its mobile number portability reform. The change was modest on paper: customers could keep their phone numbers when switching networks, and transfers had to complete within hours rather than days. Yet the outcome was immediate and measurable. Within a year, according to Ofcom's 2004 market report, churn between operators increased sharply, average contract lock-ins shortened, and smaller providers gained meaningful market share for the first time. One regulatory tweak altered an entire industry's power balance—not by dictating prices or mandating behaviour, but by lowering the cost of exit. Interoperability was the quiet lever behind that shift.

The parallel to digital money is not metaphorical but structural. Open standards disarm monopolies. Portability disciplines incumbents. Transparent interfaces enable competition on service rather than capture. A CBDC that relies on proprietary pipes or exclusive wallet providers risks repeating the pre-2003 telecoms world, where switching costs made customer loyalty indistinguishable from customer confinement. The essential question echoes through every architecture debate: will public money remain contestable, or will convenience drift into lock-in?

The first claim starts with the architecture of *open APIs*. *Show*: in September 2018, the European Union implemented the Second Payment Services Directive (PSD2), forcing banks to provide secure, standardised interfaces to licensed third parties. *Name*: European Commission, PSD2, effective January 2018 with enforcement ramping through 2019. *Explain*: PSD2 eliminated banks' exclusive control over account data by mandating open technical access. This allowed fintechs like Tink and TrueLayer to offer account aggregation, budgeting tools, and payment initiation without requiring customers to abandon their existing banks. *Implication*: open APIs turn a closed financial silo into a competitive field. They separate the provision of infrastructure from the provision of services.

Metrics illustrate the shift. After PSD2 implementation, the European Banking Authority recorded thousands of daily API calls within months; by 2020, volumes ran into the millions. Behaviour changed accordingly: customers began piecing together financial services from multiple providers rather than relying on a single institution. The infrastructure became a platform, not a fortress.

A CBDC without open APIs would invert this logic. If the only way to hold or spend digital sovereign money is through a single official app, competition dies at the moment of launch. If access is intermediated only by banks on exclusive terms, CBDC becomes a captive channel for incumbents rather than an engine of innovation.

Open standards, therefore, are not a courtesy. They are a constitutional requirement for contestability.

The motif of *the door* threads through this section. An open door invites choice; a closed door chooses for you.

The second claim concerns *reference wallets*. *Show*: in 2011, the World Wide Web Consortium (W3C) adopted HTML5 as a formal standard after years of browser fragmentation. *Name*: W3C Recommendation, October 2014 for the final specification, but functional alignment began much earlier. *Explain*: once a common reference implementation emerged—clean, predictable, documented—browser vendors could differentiate through performance and design rather than proprietary markup. *Implication*: a reference wallet for CBDCs, openly published and freely implementable, creates a baseline that private actors can exceed but never undermine.

This matters because money interfaces tend to ossify. If a single private wallet becomes the dominant gateway to a CBDC, its design choices—fee structures, default behaviours, data-sharing patterns—become de facto public policy without public consent. A reference wallet establishes a public benchmark: citizens can always fall back on a free, audited, feature-complete option, and competitors must justify their deviations.

A counter-example clarifies the limits. *Show*: India's Unified Payments Interface (UPI), launched by the National Payments Corporation of India in April 2016, does not impose a single reference wallet. Instead, it relies on voluntary adoption across competing apps. *Explain*: the absence of a reference implementation has not hindered adoption—UPI became one of the world's fastest-growing payment systems. *Implication*: reference wallets are not always necessary for a competitive ecosystem, especially when incumbents are cooperative and regulatory pressure ensures interoperability.

Reconciliation matters. Unlike UPI, a CBDC carries constitutional stakes. The interface to public money must be auditable, durable, and guaranteed. A reference wallet does not stifle innovation; it anchors it.

The third claim turns to *portability*. The telecom analogy is exact, not poetic. *Show*: Australia introduced mobile number portability in September 2001. A 2002 Australian Communications Authority report found that within months, portability increased competitive pressure and encouraged new entry. *Explain*: portability removes switching friction by ensuring customers do not lose their identifier. *Implication*: CBDC wallets should adopt the same principle—users should be able to migrate their balances, transaction histories (where lawful), credentials, and personalised settings between providers with minimal cost and no behavioural penalty.

Portability is visible behaviour. A customer who can switch providers in minutes exercises genuine choice. A customer who cannot switch because their employer mandates a specific wallet, or because their transaction history cannot migrate, is not loyal—they are trapped.

The motif of *the door* returns: portability is the hinge that allows the door to move.

A plausible counter-argument warns that portability could weaken security. Migrating wallet credentials between providers might introduce attack surfaces. The limitation is real. Yet this concern is reconcilable. Secure migration protocols—cryptographic proofs, hardware-bound attestations, regulated transfer windows—allow safe portability without exposing private keys. The telecom analogy again helps: number portability required coordination, verification, and timed releases, but these challenges were solvable. Complexity is not an excuse for lock-in.

The fourth claim concerns *open standards for programmability*. *Show*: in June 2022, the Monetary Authority of Singapore launched Project Orchid, exploring programmable money with standardised interfaces. *Name*: MAS, Project Orchid (November 2022 report). *Explain*: by defining common instruction formats for conditional payments, MAS ensured that multiple wallet providers could build compatible features without proprietary scripts. *Implication*: openness in programmability prevents fragmentation, ensuring that public money behaves consistently across providers.

The risk of closed programmability is simple: a fragmented ecosystem where some wallets support certain rules and others do not. That fragmentation is not innovation. It is confusion masquerading as progress. A CBDC must behave identically regardless of who provides the wallet. Only then can competition focus on design, support, and user experience rather than artificial compatibility moats.

The final claim concerns *contestability as governance*. Open standards are not merely technical preferences; they are political safeguards. When systems are interoperable, no actor—public or private—can dominate by default. Contestability disciplines both state and market.

A second example illustrates this equilibrium. *Show*: the UK's Open Banking Standard, launched in 2016, created a governance framework that balanced regulatory authority with industry engagement. *Name*: Open Banking Implementation Entity (OBIE), established 2016. *Explain*: the framework required transparency, published specifications, and periodic public consultations. *Implication*: open standards work best when backed by procedural guarantees, not discretionary goodwill.

A counter-example again clarifies the stakes. Closed digital ID systems in several countries have created effective monopolies for authentication. The limitation is that such systems often begin as convenience upgrades but end as mandatory infrastructure. Reconciliation for CBDCs requires explicit protections: standardised APIs, portability rights, multiple wallet providers, and transparent governance of changes.

The unresolved tension that must close this subchapter concerns the future shape of digital money: should the state provide the rails but never the gate? Should private providers compete on services but never on access? Should portability be instantaneous or conditional? Should reference wallets be mandatory to publish or merely optional to use? And the deepest question: what level of openness is sufficient to ensure that public money never becomes a private bottleneck?

The door is built either way. The choice is whether it stays open.

Chapter 6
The Wallet Is the Constitution

A few years ago, a software update in a widely-used mobile payment app quietly altered its default privacy setting. Overnight, millions of users found their contact networks cross-referenced, their spending patterns categorised, and their routine transactions enrolled in a behaviour-prediction model they had never knowingly agreed to. Nothing dramatic happened at first; no alarms sounded, no scandals erupted. But something deeper had shifted. Rights that looked sturdy in legislation dissolved into preference panes and toggles. A constitution had been re-written in code—not by lawmakers, but by a silent update that nobody voted for.

This quiet episode tells us something essential about digital money. We often imagine that the constitution of a financial system lives in statutes, regulatory frameworks, parliamentary debates, and judicial precedents. Yet with a retail digital currency—one accessed primarily through a user-facing wallet—the constitution migrates into the interface. Rights are granted or withdrawn not merely by policy but by the behaviour of the client: what it records, what it reveals, what it permits, what it nudges. The deeper paradox is that the most important legal safeguards may be the ones that appear not as clauses in legislation but as constraints in code.

Every society that experiments with sovereign digital money faces this inversion. The site of power is no longer only the ledger; it is the terminal in the citizen's hand. The design of that device—how it manages keys, how it asks for consent, how it flags risk, how it recovers access—determines whether a CBDC behaves like cash, like a bank account, or like a tracking system. Technical choices here translate directly into social outcomes: autonomy or paternalism; privacy or exposure; independence or dependency. The wallet becomes the boundary between the citizen and the state, between dignity and data extraction.

What makes this boundary fragile is how easy it is to shift without notice. A client's behaviour can change by deployer fiat: a new set of analytics, a re-ordered menu, a redesigned permissions prompt.

Small frictions can channel users from private modes into monitored rails. A security upgrade can, if mis-specified, become a surveillance upgrade. And the most consequential risks rarely arrive in dramatic form. They creep in through what designers call "dark patterns"—defaults that track rather than shield, flows that steer rather than present genuine choice, recovery paths that offer convenience at the cost of undue centralisation.

This chapter therefore begins with agency: the power of the user's own device. A CBDC wallet must enforce the rights that matter in practice—control over private keys, authentic consent, accessible interfaces, safeguards that respect diverse capabilities and household structures. Parental controls, for example, can empower guardians without normalising intrusive oversight; accessibility features can widen financial inclusion without turning vulnerability into data exposure. *Client power*, in this context, is not a slogan. It is the first guarantee of a constitutional digital currency.

Privacy follows the same logic. Promises are not enough. A trustworthy system must embody privacy in how the wallet works by default: performing sensitive checks locally where possible, revealing only what is necessary, using selective disclosure rather than full data dumps, and maintaining genuine anonymity for low-value payments. A constitution worthy of the name is one that citizens experience in their everyday transactions, not only in official statements.

We then confront the tension between usability and manipulation. Nudges are inevitable in any interface, but the stakes are higher where money is concerned. If a user is funnelled toward fully traceable modes while private pathways are buried three taps away, their autonomy becomes performative rather than real. The line between suggestion and coercion can be thin, especially when the system is designed by institutions with political or commercial interests. Genuine consent must be reversible, comprehensible, and logged in a way that cannot be retroactively rewritten.

The most delicate part of the wallet's constitution concerns recovery. People lose devices. Households face bereavement. Keys fail. These moments expose the fragility of purely technical safeguards. They also tempt policymakers toward centralised backdoors that create more problems than they solve. A resilient CBDC must offer recovery mechanisms—time-delayed social recovery, offline credentials, inheritance frameworks—that protect against accidental loss without opening structural vulnerabilities or secret override functions.

Threaded throughout is a recurring motif: the wallet as a civic instrument. It sits closer to the citizen than any bank branch or statute. It mediates daily financial life in ways no regulator can fully oversee. It is therefore the place where rights are either respected or eroded, often without fanfare. Treat the wallet casually, and the constitution becomes a matter of convenience. Treat it seriously, and it becomes a guardian of everyday freedoms.

The stakes should feel familiar. We have seen analogous battles before—in browsers that shape the open web, in mobile operating systems that govern app ecosystems, in messaging platforms that define norms of privacy and speech. With a CBDC, the consequences stretch further. If the interface narrows the user's horizon, the entire system contracts. If the interface empowers, the entire system gains legitimacy.

What this chapter offers is a map of the fault lines. Not theoretical tensions, but practical ones: where agency meets paternalism; where privacy meets compliance; where safety meets overreach; where convenience meets constitutional drift. By the end, the reader will see the wallet not as a technical accessory but as the living front line of public money.

The constitutional question is no longer abstract: who, exactly, writes the rules you experience when you tap to pay? And more provocatively, how do you ensure those rules serve you—even when nobody is watching?

Client power and user agency: Shows why the wallet enforces rights in practice. Discusses key management, parental controls, and accessibility.

In April 2022, the Reserve Bank of India released a post-incident note describing how a single configuration error in a major mobile payments platform had locked thousands of users out of their accounts in Chandigarh within minutes. The fault was mundane: a permissions mismatch pushed through a routine update. Yet for several hours, people could neither pay for bus fares nor retrieve balances. No law had changed. No regulation had been rewritten. But the lived constitution of their money—what they could do, what they could authorise, what they could access—shifted because a client update said so. Rights that looked stable on paper proved volatile in users' hands. The incident presented a quiet lesson: where digital money is concerned, the locus of agency sits as much in the interface as in the statute.

This tension becomes sharper in a CBDC architecture, where the user-facing wallet often defines the boundary between autonomy and dependency. A citizen does not experience rights through parliamentary debates or regulatory handbooks. They experience them in the moment they tap a button, restore a backup, or decline a disclosure request. The client dictates the front line of consent. It shapes the rhythms of daily financial life: how quickly a parent can set spending limits for a teenager; whether an elder with low vision can authenticate without assistance; whether a migrant worker with a basic handset can transact without sharing more information than necessary. The practical constitution of a CBDC is not an abstract idea. It is a screen, a prompt, a key, an action.

The simplest place to see this constitution in motion is key management. Cryptographic keys anchor control in a digital money system; whoever holds them can spend, approve, and prove ownership. In 2021, the Monetary Authority of Singapore tested a prototype wallet that allowed users to store private keys in a secure enclave chip, isolating them from the operating system. The design showed what agency looks like when embedded properly: the user, rather than the platform, held the final authority to release signing power. The system "showed" this principle through its behaviour:

no back-end function could unilaterally move funds. Naming the design choice—hardware-bound keys—made clear what it accomplished. It anchored sovereignty at the edge. The implication is profound. If a CBDC wallet shifts key control even a small distance upstream, agency dissolves. A central service capable of overriding keys, even for seemingly benign purposes, becomes an unseen constitutional amendment.

Yet the counter-example deserves equal weight. In 2020, during pilot studies in Shenzhen, millions of digital yuan wallets relied on cloud recovery tied to national ID numbers. The approach reduced the risk of permanent loss but created a central pivot of control: a single authority could, at least in principle, reset access. The limitation here is not theoretical. A centralised reset pathway introduces an attack surface and, more subtly, an imbalance of power. Reconciling this requires careful design: recovery mechanisms that work without granting one institution the unilateral ability to impersonate the user.

Threaded through these design tensions is a recurring motif: *the edge is where freedom lives*. The closer control sits to the user's own device, the sturdier their rights become. The further it drifts toward central servers, the more fragile those rights appear.

Beyond keys, the wallet must express agency in the texture of everyday controls. Parental oversight offers a revealing case. When Denmark's National Bank explored retail digital cash prototypes in 2021, researchers highlighted how parents used ad hoc pocket-money arrangements that combined autonomy with guidance: a teen could buy a snack on the way home but could not empty the household budget. A CBDC wallet that mirrors this nuance—time-limited allowances, merchant-category ceilings, adjustable permissions—can strengthen family-level governance without importing heavy-handed surveillance. The behaviour is visible: a young person tapping to pay for lunch sees their allowed balance, not a dossier of their past purchases. The question becomes whether the wallet treats youth autonomy as a feature to be supported or a vulnerability to be exploited. The former builds trust. The latter erodes it.

Accessibility extends the same theme into a broader social contract. Digital payments already exclude millions through tiny design oversights: text too small, gestures too precise, languages too scarce. In 2023, the UK's Financial Conduct Authority found that 14% of adults with disabilities reported difficulty authenticating online due to interface complexity. This is not a trivial figure; it is a civic warning. If a CBDC wallet is to function as public infrastructure, it must accommodate diverse bodies, devices, and contexts. That means predictable navigation for cognitive impairments, audio output for low vision, vibration cues for hearing loss, and offline tokens for those with intermittent connectivity. The "show → name → explain → implication" chain here is stark. When an interface excludes, exclusion becomes systemic. When it includes, it expands the public sphere of finance.

Another dimension of agency lies in the wallet's responses to information requests. Consent that cannot be refused is not consent. A user who sees a pop-up labelled "required for security" is rarely presented with nuance. Yet small behaviours reveal the deeper structure: whether granular permissions exist; whether the interface explains *why* data is requested; whether the user can transact privately at low values without unlocking excessive flows of information. These decisions belong to constitutional engineering. If the wallet compresses choice into a single disclosure pathway, the system will accumulate unnecessary data. If it offers meaningful branching, users can calibrate their privacy without sacrificing safety.

A credible counter-example illustrates how fragile this balance is. In the Netherlands in 2019, a major bank attempted to bundle behavioural analytics into its payments app, requiring customers to accept data-sharing to use certain features. Public backlash halted the initiative within days. The episode underscored a central limitation: interfaces that place convenience behind a wall of compelled consent cannot sustain public legitimacy. Reconciling the tension requires explicit, logged, reversible consent flows that cannot be silently overwritten in future updates.

The wallet must also insulate users from institutional asymmetries. A system where support staff, contractors, or third-party integrators can trigger forced logouts or alter permission states introduces a subtle but consequential imbalance. In contrast, architectures that log every administrative action—and require multi-party authorisation for sensitive operations—signal a commitment to procedural fairness. Behaviour makes this visible: users who recover access after a device loss can inspect the cryptographic trail that restored their rights, rather than relying on opaque assurances.

Threading back to the motif, *the edge is where freedom lives*, recovery provides the most delicate test. People will forget passwords, drop phones, and navigate bereavement. A constitutional wallet must offer pathways that safeguard property without creating systemic override functions. Social recovery with time delays—friends or family approving access after a wait—offers one scenario. Multi-device quorum approval is another. What matters is that no single institution holds the unilateral ability to reconstruct identity. The implication is clear. The integrity of a CBDC depends as much on its recovery model as on its encryption.

Agency also intersects with cultural and linguistic realities. A migrant arriving in Berlin with a basic handset faces different constraints to a retiree in Glasgow using a tablet. The wallet must detect and adapt to these contexts: caching instructions locally in the user's primary language; offering large-type modes; allowing offline proofs for small-value transactions. When the interface respects the diversity of users' lived circumstances, it becomes a civic tool, not an administrative gatekeeper.

All these features—key management, parental controls, accessibility, consent, recovery—might look like technical details. They are constitutional details. They determine whether the user stands as the primary agent or the passive endpoint of a centralised system. They measure the distance between the promise of a CBDC and its practice.

And so the unresolved tension remains: when the next update arrives, who truly controls the device that controls the money?

Privacy by default, not promise: Argues for default local processing, selective disclosure, and transaction limits that preserve anonymity for small payments

In January 2023, Europe's data protection authorities published a joint statement criticising a proposal from a major payments processor in Frankfurt to expand behavioural analytics across its merchant terminals. The plan would have linked low-value card transactions—coffee purchases, bus fares, small grocery bills—to individual customer profiles, creating a dataset capable of tracing daily routines with forensic precision. Nothing in the system required this detail; the company argued it would "improve service personalisation". Yet the backlash was immediate. German regulators warned that "proportionality cannot be retrofitted," and the proposal was shelved within weeks. The episode illustrated a simple truth: privacy that relies on good intentions or policy declarations, rather than structural design, fails at the moment pressures rise.

For CBDCs, the stakes are higher still. A digital currency that merely promises privacy mirrors the card networks that citizens already mistrust. A CBDC that *enforces* privacy—locally, silently, predictably—becomes a different kind of civic instrument. Privacy by default is not sentiment. It is a technical stance. It asks that sensitive checks occur on the device rather than on a server; that only the minimum necessary facts leave the user's hand; that small transactions remain genuinely anonymous without backdoor reconstruction. The wallet becomes a shield rather than a funnel. And in practice, that shield is built not through rhetoric, but through a sequence of behaviours: what data stays local, what disclosures are partial, what limits define the private sphere.

The logic of local processing appears stark when contrasted with real-world failures. In 2020, the Norwegian Consumer Council published a detailed analysis showing how dozens of mobile apps transmitted precise user locations—down to three decimal places of longitude—to advertising exchanges. Users relied on privacy "promises" that proved hollow. What mattered was design: the data left the device before the user exercised any agency. The case "shows" the risk: privacy that depends on personal vigilance is already lost. Naming the issue—server-side over-collection—clarifies the structural flaw. The implication for CBDCs is unavoidable. If sensitive eligibility checks, merchant-type validations, or low-value anonymity rules are executed remotely, then privacy exists only as long as the server's operators choose to honour restraint.

Local processing reverses this dependency. A wallet can verify that a payment is below an anonymity threshold without sending the value upstream; it can confirm device integrity without exposing identifiers; it can generate proofs that a transaction meets legal requirements without revealing the underlying data. Zero-knowledge techniques, selective disclosure, and hardware-bound secure elements are not academic toys. They are privacy's working machinery. They bind the system's operators to a narrow field of vision, regardless of future political incentives.

Selective disclosure builds on the same motif—*proportionality baked into the edge*. Consider how the European Digital Identity Wallet pilots in 2022 allowed citizens to prove they were over 18 without exposing name, address, or full date of birth. The principle translated cleanly: reveal only what the counterparty needs to know. In a CBDC, the equivalent might be proving that a payment falls within a permitted merchant category without exposing a transaction history. Show a fact; withhold the narrative. The behaviour matters. When a user pays for public transport, the system should confirm "valid fare" rather than transmit a full string of identifiers.

Yet a credible limitation deserves attention. Selective disclosure systems can fail when poorly implemented. During the early US "Real ID" rollouts (2005–2011), several states attempted to build digital identity systems with granular disclosures but ended up centralising citizen data in large, breach-prone databases. The limitation here is not the concept but the architecture: selective disclosure becomes meaningless if all attributes are stored in a single, queryable store. Reconciling the tension requires a structural rule: store less, fragment what remains, and tie disclosure to verifiable, on-device proofs rather than bulk server look-ups.

The third pillar—anonymous small-value payments—brings privacy down to earth. Cash has long provided a zone of social autonomy: the ability to buy a newspaper, tip a waiter, or make a modest donation without leaving a broadcast trace. For digital systems to honour that civic space, anonymity thresholds must be real, not symbolic. They must prevent reconstruction through side channels, correlation attacks, or metadata leaks. In 2021, the European Central Bank's research group explored offline-capable, low-value CBDC transactions that used device-to-device settlement with spent-token tracking that revealed no identity at the point of exchange. The "show" here lies in the design behaviour: the system treated anonymity for under-50-euro payments as a default rather than an exception. Naming the method—value-based pseudonymity—clarified the approach. The implication was political as much as technical: privacy was protected by making low-value anonymity less work than tracing, not more.

Still, anonymity thresholds create an inherent tension. Too low, and meaningful privacy disappears. Too high, and policymakers fear creating blind spots for illicit finance. The credible counter-example appears in the United Kingdom's experience with prepaid cards before 2010. Generous anonymous limits enabled a niche of criminal misuse. But the lesson was subtler: regulators responded by tightening limits without dismantling the entire category. Reconciling this history with CBDCs requires a calibrated approach: anonymous zones sized to support civic life, paired with fast, judge-issued warrants for investigations above those thresholds. Privacy at the bottom end; due process at the top.

Threading the motif again—*proportionality baked into the edge*—reveals the deeper constitutional logic. Privacy cannot depend on a central authority's restraint. It must depend on the fact that the authority does not receive unnecessary data in the first place. A CBDC that streams every transaction to a central ledger for "analysis" recreates the surveillance dynamics of card networks, only with greater precision. A CBDC that processes thresholds locally in the user's hands transforms the balance: institutions receive exactly what they are entitled to, no more.

This raises another important behavioural signal. If a user must navigate multiple menus to activate private mode, but only one tap to expose their full transaction flow, the system nudges them toward transparency, not autonomy. Dark pattern research—from Harry Brignull's early cataloguing in 2010 to the Norwegian Consumer Council's 2021 "Deceived by Design" report—shows that defaults dominate behaviour. A meaningful CBDC must therefore adopt a strict rule: privacy should be the default pathway for low-value payments, not a buried option. The interface must *resist* over-disclosure, not encourage it.

To ground this further, consider Taiwan's EasyCard system, which has provided low-value, offline public transit payments since 2002. The behaviour is telling. When a commuter taps into the metro, the state does not receive a name. It receives a fare validation. The card reveals only what is necessary. This modest infrastructure demonstrates how default anonymity for minor transactions can persist for decades without undermining legitimate oversight. The CBDC equivalent is more complex, but the underlying logic—minimal revelation—remains sound.

The risk of relying on privacy "promises" rather than default design becomes acute when incentives shift. Political transitions, fiscal crises, or security scares can tempt governments to broaden data capture. If privacy protections live only in policy documents, they are easy targets. If they live in local processing, limits, and proofs, they are far harder to erode without public scrutiny. Design becomes a constitutional safeguard.

A structural counter-weight is also needed: independent verification. Privacy-protecting designs cannot remain proprietary black boxes. Civil-society cryptographers, academic auditors, and consumer protection agencies must be able to inspect reference wallets, confirm proof systems, and test disclosure pathways. Without this transparency, privacy-by-default risks becoming privacy-by-marketing.

A final example sharpens the stakes. In 2022, during post-hurricane recovery in Puerto Rico, several banks temporarily suspended card authorisation systems due to network outages. People with cash managed. People with digital wallets lost autonomy—precisely because the wallets depended on upstream checks. A CBDC that treats privacy as default must also treat autonomy as default: offline capability for low-value transactions, proof-of-validity without proof-of-identity, and a local fallback that mirrors the resilience of cash. The motif appears again: privacy and autonomy arise together when the edge carries weight.

All this leads to an unresolved question that sits at the heart of CBDC design: if privacy must be enforced by default, which institution guarantees that defaults cannot be silently rewritten?

Human factors and dark patterns: Identifies nudges that funnel users into tracked modes. Recommends consent that is real, reversible, and logged

In May 2021, the Norwegian Consumer Council published *Deceived by Design*, a forensic report detailing how major technology firms—Facebook, Google, Microsoft—steered millions of Europeans toward data-sharing options they had not meaningfully chosen. The Council's researchers replicated registration flows in Oslo and recorded a consistent pattern: privacy-preserving choices were buried in expanded menus, framed negatively, or paired with warnings implying loss of functionality. In one striking example, declining personalised ads required navigating three additional screens, while accepting them demanded a single tap. The outcome was measurable: acceptance rates surged when friction favoured disclosure. The lesson was not about advertising. It was about architecture. People behave differently when the system tilts the floor beneath their feet.

CBDC wallets can tilt the floor just as easily. A default mode that logs merchant categories, device identifiers, or geolocation can be "accepted" by millions simply because the alternative is harder to find. A pop-up requesting expanded permissions can be framed as essential to security. A consent screen can blur distinctions between what is optional and what is legally required. And when public money is involved—when the instrument mediating daily transactions operates under sovereign authority—dark patterns acquire constitutional weight. Nudges become governance.

To understand how these mechanics translate to financial behaviour, start with a simple observation. In 2019, researchers at the University of Chicago analysed online mortgage applications and found that applicants were 15% more likely to accept higher-fee options when the low-fee path required multiple clicks. The "show" here is behavioural. People follow the path of least resistance. Naming the pattern—choice architecture bias—helps clarify how subtle design shapes real-world decisions. The implication for CBDC design is immediate: if private pathways require more friction than tracked pathways, privacy becomes an illusion wrapped in a user interface.

The motif running through this argument is simple and quiet: *the floor tilts.* A design that seems neutral can slope toward disclosure. A wallet that presents an effortless "recommended" mode may normalise traceability. A toggle that resets after an update can convert yesterday's private choice into today's monitored one. When the floor tilts, people slide.

Dark patterns emerge in three primary behaviours, all visible in existing digital systems. The first is *obstruction*: privacy options buried behind irrelevant menus. The second is *pressure*: language that warns users they might "lose access" or "reduce security" if they decline additional telemetry. The third is *default capture*: the reversion of settings after updates. Each appears trivial to a designer. Each becomes consequential when applied to a sovereign digital currency.

A 2020 investigation by the UK Information Commissioner's Office found that several children's apps installed in London primary schools defaulted to location tracking unless a parent opted out—a process that required navigating six screens. The "limitation" emerging here is educational: many parents lacked the time or fluency to override the default. CBDCs will confront similar asymmetries. A wallet deployed nationwide must accommodate users who have limited technical confidence, low literacy, or cognitive impairments. If privacy requires vigilance, privacy fails. Reconciling this limitation demands structural safeguards: defaults must favour maximal protection, especially for vulnerable groups.

Two historical examples illustrate the stakes. First, the design of the UK's GOV.UK Verify system between 2016 and 2019. Though intended to give citizens control over identity attributes, the flow often channelled users into high-disclosure verification routes because they looked simpler. A second example appears in India's Aadhaar-linked payments ecosystem. Field studies in Karnataka (2018) showed that users frequently authorised unnecessary biometric checks because declining required re-authentication under uncertain conditions. These cases "show" how users interpret uncertainty as risk, leading them to over-comply. Naming this behaviour—risk asymmetry in interface design—helps clarify why nudges matter. The implication for CBDC wallets is clear: any ambiguity will push users toward traceable modes.

A credible counter-example also matters. Estonia's e-identity system, introduced in 2002, took a different path. It provided clear, unambiguous consent prompts, local cryptographic signing, and independent audit trails. Citizens could view—and challenge—any instance of government access. The limitation of Estonia's model lies in its dependence on high digital literacy and strong state capacity, not easily reproducible everywhere. Reconciling this requires adapting the underlying principle—transparent, user-verifiable logs—even where state infrastructure is less mature.

The issue becomes constitutional when silent updates enter the picture. A CBDC wallet may require regular upgrades for security, but these upgrades can smuggle behavioural changes. Imagine a wallet where the "private mode" for low-value payments becomes slightly harder to access after an update, or where merchant categories are suddenly pre-authorised for analytics. The behaviour is subtle; the effect is profound. Once again, the floor tilts. A public-money system cannot rely on private vigilance to police such shifts. It needs structural obligations: update diff logs, version histories, non-repudiable notices, and a right to roll back non-security-related changes. Consent must be logged in a way that user and regulator can verify independently.

The social consequences of ignoring human factors are visible in other domains. In 2021, WhatsApp attempted to modify its data-sharing terms. Although the company insisted the changes were benign, the consent screen framed refusal as a threat to continued use. Millions of users migrated to Signal and Telegram, not because they read the fine print but because the dark pattern signalled disrespect. Trust collapsed through interface behaviour, not policy text. A CBDC that mishandles consent risks a wider legitimacy failure. Public money cannot afford a WhatsApp moment.

To prevent such collapse, consent must meet three criteria: it must be *real*, meaning the user understands and freely chooses; it must be *reversible*, allowing the user to withdraw without penalty; it must be *logged*, preserving an independent record of what was agreed. These behaviours protect autonomy in practice. They transform consent from a gesture into a verifiable act.

Threading the motif once more—*the floor tilts*—helps illuminate a broader warning. A CBDC does not need malicious intent to erode agency. All it needs is an interface that drifts over time. Defaults slide. Menus lengthen. Buttons shrink. Permissions toggle. And users, pressed by routine, follow the slope.

The unresolved question is therefore stark: will the sovereign digital wallet be designed to tilt toward autonomy or toward surveillance?

Recovery without surveillance: Designs for lost devices and inheritance that avoid centralised backdoors. Example: social recovery with time delays

On 12 September 2020, the founders of Argent, a London-based smart-contract wallet, published a post-mortem detailing an unusual rescue. A user had lost access to their phone and forgotten their recovery phrase, yet the wallet was restored—legitimately—through a quorum of trusted "guardians". These guardians, which could include friends, devices, or institutions, each approved a recovery request. Only after a mandatory delay did the wallet regenerate new keys. There was no master password stored on a server in London or San Francisco. No engineer could override the process. The system relied on protocol, not privilege, and the outcome was concrete: a recovered wallet with no centralised backdoor unlocked. The recovery was slow by design. The slowness protected the user.

The paradox that haunts sovereign digital money is this: the safer a recovery mechanism becomes for the forgetful or bereaved, the more dangerous it becomes if centralised. A CBDC environment cannot rely on the old banking fallback—customer service agents resetting passwords after verifying an ID document—because that pathway creates the very backdoor the system must resist. If one official can flip a switch, so can an attacker. So can an insider. So can a future government with shifting priorities. The challenge is to engineer recovery in a way that honours human fragility without granting institutional omnipotence. People lose devices. People die. The question is not whether recovery is needed. It is whether recovery can be engineered without surveillance or unilateral control.

The central motif is *the slow door*: recovery that opens, but only through layered, transparent delay. A slow door resists coercion. It resists insider malice. It resists the panicked shortcut. And in resisting, it expresses a principle: user agency must outlive the device itself.

The first major claim is that recovery must be decentralised. A system where a central bank or treasury can reassign a wallet's keys after receiving a request creates a single point of failure. To "show" the danger, consider the 2014 compromise of the US Office of Personnel Management, where records for 21.5 million federal employees were exfiltrated. The breach was not a consequence of weak cryptography; it was a consequence of central aggregation. Naming the pattern—administrative concentration—helps explain why CBDC recovery must avoid creating privileged databases of reset keys or override credentials. The implication is that recovery must flow through multiple independent actors who cannot collude instantly.

Social-recovery mechanisms illustrate this principle. When implemented in Singapore's OpenCerts project in 2019, guardianship models enabled institutions to validate lost educational credentials without storing the underlying keys. Users regained functionality through distributed verification rather than central intervention. The system "measured" trust not in access but in thresholds: two of three guardians, three of five, or other quorums. CBDC wallets can adopt similar logic for key regeneration, ensuring that no single actor—public or private—can seize control.

A counter-example strengthens the argument. Apple's 2023 introduction of Advanced Data Protection brought end-to-end encryption to iCloud backups, but recovery still depended on either a passcode or a recovery contact. If both were compromised, the device could be seized silently. The limitation here is structural: the convenience of seamless cloud syncing created a central point where compromised passcodes could cascade into total loss. Reconciling this limitation requires designing CBDC wallets where device loss does not imply identity loss, and where identity loss does not imply recoverability by a singular authority.

The second claim concerns inheritance. Traditional estates rely on probate courts, executors, and occasionally banks that maintain dormant accounts for years. CBDCs risk automating inheritance in ways that reveal sensitive transaction histories or personal metadata. The wallet itself must mediate the transition without exposing the ledger to scrutiny. To "show" the contours, consider how Norway's digital postbox system (2016) implemented time-locked access for next-of-kin notifications. Access required multi-step authentication and strict minimisation: executors could see only what was legally relevant. Naming the principle—selective disclosure—highlights its relevance. The implication is that CBDC inheritance flows must expose balances or recovery pathways, not behavioural histories.

Time delays play an essential role. A delay is not a bureaucratic inconvenience but a defence against coercion. If a compromised guardian attempts a fraudulent recovery, the victim gains time to react. If heirs disagree, the wallet can require reconciliation before triggering transfer. Time, in this context, is a security parameter. A 48-hour or 7-day delay provides a behavioural buffer: it shifts power away from whoever holds the device and toward whoever legitimately owns the value.

The slow door motif returns here. A system that opens instantly might seem efficient, but efficiency in recovery is often the enemy of integrity. The door must resist being opened by anyone who shouts the loudest.

The third claim is that local hardware still matters. Secure elements, found in smartphones and smartcards, allow keys to remain offline even when the device interacts with the network. If a CBDC wallet stores its primary keys in such hardware, then recovery processes can regenerate new keys without anyone—central bank, wallet provider, or malicious actor—ever seeing the originals. This behaviour embodies minimisation: privacy preserved by the simple fact that sensitive material never leaves the device. To "name" the design principle—hardware-rooted isolation—helps clarify why secure elements are not optional enhancements but constitutional components of a sovereign wallet.

Limitations exist. Hardware can be stolen or destroyed. Secure elements can fail. The reconciliation lies in layered resilience: multi-device recovery, guardian-based restoration, and time-locked transfers for inheritance, all orchestrated without central override.

Real-world examples illustrate how such layers operate under pressure. In 2018, during the floods in Kerala, India, offline Aadhaar authentication stations were compromised or unusable. Yet families regained access to government payments because a distributed set of local officials could attest to identities through quorum-based verification. The "behaviour" here was decentralised attestation under stress. The implication is that recovery systems must function when infrastructure does not—precisely when centralised backdoors would be most tempting. A CBDC designed for crises must avoid such temptation structurally.

The final claim is that recovery must be observable by the user. Every step—guardian approvals, time delays, device registration—must generate logs that the user can verify. Logs cannot depend on cloud storage, which would reintroduce surveillance risk. Instead, they can be anchored cryptographically on the device or on a privacy-preserving bulletin board. Naming this principle—verifiable transparency—clarifies its purpose: it renders covert recovery impossible. The implication is that users can detect interference even if they cannot prevent attempts.

Threading the motif once more: *the slow door protects.* A door that opens only with distributed consent, with delay, with selective disclosure, with local cryptography, cannot be forced silently. It protects not through secrecy but through structure.

The unresolved tension sits at the heart of the design. How slow should the slow door be? Slow enough to resist coercion, fast enough to support urgent need. Distributed enough to prevent misuse, simple enough for non-technical citizens to understand. Every parameter—quorum size, delay duration, visibility—encodes a constitutional value.

The decision ahead is stark and inescapable: will recovery in a sovereign digital currency rely on trust in institutions, or trust in protocols that even institutions cannot unilaterally violate?

Chapter 7
Economic Levers in Code

At the height of the pandemic in April 2020, the United States Treasury sent more than 80 million stimulus payments in a single week—an extraordinary feat of administrative delivery, yet one that still left millions waiting. Some cheques went astray. Some bank transfers bounced. Some households waited months. The episode revealed something deeper than logistical strain: monetary policy had the will, but not the wires. The tools were powerful, yet blunt. They worked at scale but stumbled at the edges where timing, tailoring, and trust mattered most. That gap—between macroeconomic intent and real-world execution—is where a programmable public currency enters the debate.

The idea is disquieting and exhilarating in equal measure. What if money could carry instructions? What if interest rates could be encoded directly into a balance? What if a payment could settle only when a specific condition was met? These questions feel almost heretical because they challenge a century-long assumption that economic levers sit in marble buildings, not in smartphone wallets. Yet they also reveal a tension that has haunted policymakers since the dawn of modern central banking: the need to act quickly without eroding predictability; the desire to target precisely without slipping into discrimination; the ambition to expand capability without hollowing out the financial system that supports it. Programmability makes these tensions explicit. Code renders them visible.

But visibility does not guarantee legitimacy. If anything, it sharpens the stakes. A CBDC that can adjust its own remuneration could, in principle, stimulate spending in a recession. It could also unsettle the public if the rules feel arbitrary or unfamiliar. A system that can distribute conditional subsidies could improve efficiency and fairness. It could also harden the sensation that one's economic life is subject to opaque logic. The point is not that programmable features are inherently dangerous; it is that they alter the constitutional balance between what a state may do *in theory* and what it may do *in practice*. Once the wallet becomes an instrument of policy, every parameter carries political weight.

This chapter steps directly into that territory: the domain where economics, engineering, and constitutional restraint fuse into one question—*what should money be allowed to do*? To answer it, we begin with the oldest ambition in monetary design: influencing spending behaviour. Central banks have long tweaked interest rates to manage cycles, but programmable balances shift that lever from the perimeter to the core. A wallet could, in principle, pay interest only up to a certain amount. It could allow negative rates for large, dormant holdings while shielding day-to-day balances. It could impose gentle expiry on emergency transfers to ensure they reach the real economy. The tools are familiar in spirit yet foreign in execution. The tension between stabilisation and predictability becomes tangible. Households tolerate rate changes announced on press podiums. They may bristle at rate changes delivered by client update notifications. The distinction is not only psychological; it is constitutional.

From here the chapter turns to conditionality—perhaps the most charged aspect of economic programmability. Conditional payments are not new. Governments already tie subsidies to income, location, age, or activity. Courts impose fines based on behaviour. Regulators distribute carbon credits and deduct penalties. What changes in a programmable currency is the immediacy and granularity of the mechanism. A transfer could release only when a meter reading is verified. A subsidy could diminish once a household's electricity usage crosses a threshold. A penalty could trigger when a vehicle enters a restricted zone. Each example demonstrates capability, yet each also invites a harder question: does precision empower the citizen or the issuer? Conditions that are *transparent* feel like rules. Conditions that are opaque feel like control. The difference lies in disclosure, governance, and the ability to contest outcomes. Conditionality without notice is not policy; it is code-driven coercion.

The chapter then widens to the banking system—an arena where economic levers have second-order effects. A CBDC that pays interest, or even one that feels safer than deposits, may attract funds out of commercial banks. Economists call this "disintermediation risk". Banks call it an existential threat. Yet the outcome is not preordained. Caps on holdings, tiered remuneration, or frictionless switching between CBDC and deposits can shape incentives without destabilising liquidity. What matters is the design philosophy: programmable money must not cannibalise the system that channels savings into investment. Instead, it must coexist with it—sometimes nudging, sometimes complementing, always respecting the delicate balance that keeps credit flowing.

Finally, the chapter moves beyond national borders, where programmable features confront the realities of foreign exchange, capital controls, and remittances. Imagine a worker in Leeds sending £200 to family in Manila and the funds arriving instantly as pesos at a fair conversion rate, with no predatory intermediaries siphoning value. Programmability could make such corridors trustworthy by embedding conversion rules, caps, or disclosures directly in the payment flow. Yet it could also export domestic policy preferences abroad, unintentionally framing a country's money as an instrument of influence. Interoperability could liberate or constrain. Again, the trade-off is architectural, not aspirational.

Throughout this journey runs a subtle motif: *money as choreography.* Traditional monetary tools nudge from afar; programmable tools choreograph directly. They set steps, pace, and occasionally posture. The public must understand the dance and consent to it. Without that consent, choreography becomes choreography imposed.

By the final paragraphs of this chapter, the reader will see the economic constitution of programmable money with a sharper lens. The promise is real: speed, precision, fairness, and new capabilities that improve the social contract. The peril is equally real: unpredictability, overreach, and systemic misalignment. Whether programmability becomes a stabilising force or a source of fragmentation depends entirely on how these levers are bounded, disclosed, and contested.

The question that frames what follows is simple yet profound: if money can now act, not just account—who decides the limits of its action, and how will the public keep those limits honest?

Interest, expiry, and velocity

In November 1923, as hyperinflation ravaged the Weimar Republic, the town of Schwanenkirchen in Bavaria tried an experiment. The mine owner, Max Hebecker, unable to pay workers in collapsing Reichsmarks, issued stamped scrip—*Wära*—that lost 1 per cent of its value each week unless restamped with a fee. It circulated briskly. Shops accepted it. Wages moved. The mine reopened. When Berlin banned the scheme months later, output fell and the local revival stalled. The episode survives in the economic literature as a curiosity, but it frames a real question for the present: if a currency can decay or grow by design, how far should the state choreograph its movement?

Programmable money revives this question with far greater precision. A balance can now accumulate interest at a rate specific to a user's tier. It can decay after a deadline. It can vary by circumstance. The levers that once operated only at the macro level can now reach directly into the wallet. This power sharpens an old tension. Policy needs room to manoeuvre during crises, yet households and firms need predictability to plan. When the rate on deposits changes, people grumble but understand the ritual: a central bank announces, markets react, institutions adjust. When the rate embedded in one's wallet changes overnight through an update, even if modest, the shift feels personal. Code closes the gap between policy and pocket. That proximity demands a constitutional thickness that simply did not matter when money was inert.

The first claim in this subchapter is straightforward: programmable rates can, in principle, stabilise demand more quickly than conventional tools. Show the mechanism. Imagine a CBDC whose remuneration drops gently once a balance exceeds a soft cap—say, £5,000. Name a precedent. The Bank of Japan, in January 2016, introduced a tiered negative rate system to shield household deposits while nudging institutions to deploy capital. Explain the logic. By applying interest differentials directly at the ledger level, a CBDC could replicate this tiering without burdening banks, ensuring dormant balances on retail wallets circulate during downturns. Implication: faster transmission. If every household sees spending power drift slightly when held idle, the economy gains velocity. But velocity achieved by erosion must satisfy political scrutiny that is specific, public, and contestable.

The second claim invokes expiry, a tool often caricatured yet rarely examined on its actual merits. Show the practice. China's 2022 digital yuan consumer vouchers, in Shenzhen expired after set windows, spurring measurable increases in local retail activity. Name the effect. Researchers at Peking University recorded a sharp but time-bound rise in restaurant and grocery spend. Explain the instrument. Expiry strengthens the temporal signal of policy: spend now, support the recovery. Implication: used sparingly, expiry can convert fiscal intent into real activity without raising blanket debt-financed demand. But the fairness question grows louder. A household living paycheque to paycheque may experience expiry as coercion rather than relief. A small firm that saves vouchers for inventory may lose value through no fault of its own. The line between incentive and compulsion rests on transparency, proportionality, and the option to refuse.

To test the limits of this reasoning, we need a counter-example—a case where velocity nudges did not perform as intended. India's 2016 demonetisation provides that lesson. Though not digital, it shared the spirit of forcing idle funds into use. The government withdrew high-denomination notes overnight, aiming to flush out untaxed wealth and accelerate formal transactions. The immediate effect was chaos: queues, lost income, and liquidity shortages. Consumption slumped. Small firms cut production. When replacement cash arrived months later, the velocity boost was marginal. The episode reveals what programmability cannot fix: if incentives or constraints arrive without notice or capacity to adjust, economic behaviour reflects strain, not stimulation. The reconciliation lies in design: any programmable nudge must be published, debated, and bounded. Surprise is not a policy instrument.

A recurring motif here is *the clock*. Interest accrues through time. Expiry compresses time. Velocity measures time. Each mechanism uses time as a lever. In a programmable currency, the clock becomes code. That shift invites a deeper reflection on legitimacy: who sets the clock, and how do citizens verify that the clock measures fairly?

Consider predictability. Households shape their budgets around stable expectations: rent due on the first, wages on the last, utilities mid-month. If a CBDC adjusts remuneration weekly—say, a crisis-era liquidity boost that fades as conditions improve—every change must respect those rhythms. A worker in Manchester who keeps £300 in a wallet to meet a Friday direct debit must never wake to find that balance diminished through a silent rule. Predictability is not an abstraction; it is a calendar entry. Programmable rates or expiry can fit within that calendar only if announced with the same ritualised clarity that central banks apply to interest rate decisions today.

Fairness carries similar concreteness. A pensioner in Glasgow with limited digital literacy must not be penalised by features she does not understand. If expiry boosts aggregate velocity but harms those with least flexibility, the design fails. A parent who saves digitally for school supplies must not see funds erode because the wallet misclassified them as discretionary. Programmable incentives require categorisation; categorisation introduces risk of mislabelling; mislabelling affects real households. The codification of money thus becomes the codification of judgement. That judgement must be contestable.

Programmable interest also intersects with the banking system. When a retail CBDC pays interest—especially if market-aligned—it competes with deposits. Show the behaviour. A saver moving £2,000 from a commercial bank to a CBDC wallet is not making an ideological statement; she is measuring return. Name a checkable example. The Eastern Caribbean Central Bank's DCash pilot, launched in 2021, saw modest shifts in transactional balances but no flood from banks, partly because DCash paid zero interest. Explain the mechanism. If a future CBDC offered even modest remuneration on higher tiers, funds could migrate quickly during stress. Implication: stabilisation achieved through programmable rates may destabilise the underlying financial system if not counterbalanced by caps and remuneration bands. The design must prevent a liquidity race during downturns.

These trade-offs—between stability and predictability, precision and fairness, speed and legitimacy—will shape public trust. Trust is not a slogan; it is behaviour. It is a citizen choosing the public wallet because rules feel legible. It is a merchant accepting CBDC because settlement rules remain stable across seasons. It is a student or a retiree knowing that incentives or expiry windows reflect public debate, not a policymaker's whim.

At this point the clock motif returns. The more a currency encodes time, the more time it owes the public: time for notice, time for comment, time for adjustment. A CBDC that shortens the economic cycle through expiry must lengthen the democratic cycle through consultation. Without that symmetry, velocity gains will be purchased at the cost of legitimacy.

The unresolved tension is simple and unavoidable: should money ever carry a use-by date, explicit or implicit—and if so, who decides when the clock starts and stops?

Programmable transfers and targeting

In May 2020, with Mumbai in its strictest lockdown, the Maharashtra state government launched a direct relief scheme for migrant workers who had lost access to wages and transport. The transfer—₹2,000—was small but decisive. What made the programme remarkable was the requirement that funds be spent on essentials within participating districts, enforced through merchant codes and time limits. Payments cleared rapidly, and grocery shops in Dadar and Byculla reported spikes in basic-food purchases within twenty-four hours. Yet civil-society groups, including the Mumbai-based Praja Foundation, raised concerns about exclusions: workers without Aadhaar-linked accounts or with names misspelled in databases were locked out. The scheme showed two things at once: targeting can enhance relief, and tiny errors in code or registry design can inflict real harm.

That tension—precision versus discretion—sits at the heart of programmable transfers. Conditional subsidies, earmarked support, or automated fines promise a shift from blunt fiscal tools to interventions that move at the speed of need. But the closer these rules get to the individual, the sharper the ethical edge becomes. In programmable money, discrimination is not metaphorical: it can be literal, embedded in tags, categories, exclusions, and time windows. A CBDC that executes a rule without visibility into its reasoning risks becoming a black box with sovereign force. That is why transparency matters more here than in any other layer of the system.

The first major claim begins with what programmable transfers can achieve when well designed. Show the working. Norway's electricity-bill subsidy during the winter of 2022–23 provides a baseline: households received automatic discounts when spot prices exceeded a trigger threshold, with the Norwegian Water Resources and Energy Directorate releasing monthly settlement data. While not a CBDC, the mechanism mirrors the logic programmable money could adopt—conditional relief, verified from public data, routed immediately. Name the opportunity. A CBDC could embed that threshold logic within wallets: if energy prices spike above a published benchmark, support flows automatically. Explain the benefit. There is no need for forms, queues, or retrospective claims; timing aligns with stress. Implication: households experience protection when they need it, not months later.

A second example highlights targeted subsidies. In South Korea, Gyeonggi Province deployed a youth basic income scheme in 2020, where 24-year-olds received quarterly stipends usable only within local businesses. University of Seoul researchers observed a measurable uptick in local retail turnover and an increase in small-merchant resilience. Within programmable architectures, such geographic or sectoral targeting could be implemented through merchant-category codes or regional identifiers. Explain the detail. The wallet verifies whether the merchant fits the approved category before releasing funds. Implication: policymakers gain a scalpel rather than a sledgehammer.

Yet precision exposes a danger. A credible counter-example lies in the United States' 2018 algorithmic unemployment-fraud detection system in Michigan—the MIDAS system—where automated rules incorrectly flagged over 40,000 claimants, leading to wrongful clawbacks, penalties, and in some cases bankruptcy. Though not involving digital currency, it demonstrates how rule-driven enforcement can magnify minor data errors into severe consequences. The reconciliation for CBDC design is structural: schemes that influence livelihoods must have appeals processes, logged rule histories, clear eligibility logic, and human oversight capable of reversing mistakes without stigma.

Threading through these cases is a motif: *the filter*. Every conditional transfer relies on a filter—age, postcode, income band, sector code, carbon score, household size. Filters can help, but filters can also exclude. When the filter becomes code, its operation becomes invisible to the recipient unless explicitly disclosed. The public has long tolerated broad eligibility rules for tax credits or housing benefits because those rules are legislated, debated, and printed. A programmable transfer risks turning eligibility into a silent transaction-layer verdict. If the wallet declines a purchase, the citizen should know *why*.

Conditional fines illustrate the same stakes. Show the mechanism. In Singapore, the Land Transport Authority uses automatic deductions for certain traffic offences through the CEPAS system, tagged to vehicle identity. If extended to a CBDC, a similar model could process environmental or congestion charges the instant they occur. Name the challenge. Errors in sensor data or classification would directly affect a person's balance. Explain the risk. The immediacy of settlement removes the buffer in which mistakes can be caught. Implication: auditability must be foregrounded. Every automated fine must carry a traceable identifier, an appeal path, and a reversible ledger entry.

Transparency here is not ornamental; it is constitutional. The core behaviours at stake are specific. A farmer in Kent should be able to check why a fertiliser subsidy reached her wallet on Tuesday but not on Friday. A student in Leeds should know whether a travel voucher failed because of an expired rule or an incorrect device setting. A merchant in Birmingham should see whether a rejected payment was due to a targeting constraint or a technical outage. Without such visibility, people will attribute friction to discrimination, even when the rule is benign. Perception becomes policy failure.

To avoid arbitrary outcomes, targeting logic must be both simple enough to explain and structured enough to scrutinise. Some jurisdictions already show pieces of this approach. Estonia's X-Road system, audited since 2001, logs every access to personal records; citizens can see who queried their data and when. In a CBDC context, equivalent logging could document each programmable condition evaluated during a transaction. If a subsidy is conditional on household size, the wallet could record the household-size credential checked, the rule invoked, and the decision taken, all locally visible to the user. That visibility forms the basis for contestability.

A further safeguard emerges through public rule registries. If a national treasury proposes conditional transport credits for low-income workers in Liverpool, the rules—income thresholds, merchant codes, expiry windows—should be published in a machine-readable registry with a consultation period. Economists can model impacts. Civil-society organisations can test edge cases. Technologists can find inconsistencies. This process transforms programme design from a bureaucratic box-tick to a democratic procedure. The decision to include or exclude becomes auditable before it becomes executable.

Notice how the filter motif returns. Once rules are public and testable, the filter ceases to be mysterious. And once users see filters as reasons rather than obstacles, programmable transfers begin to resemble procedural guarantees instead of privileges.

Still, a persistent tension remains. The very power that makes programmable subsidies effective—the ability to direct relief precisely where it is needed—also grants policymakers a tool that could, in less accountable hands, slide into economic steering by stealth. A grocery subsidy could become a nutritional nudge. A congestion charge could shift into a mobility score. A sectoral restriction could drift into political categorisation. The boundary between policy and profiling is thin when the filter is opaque.

So the forward test is this: if a CBDC wallet rejects a transaction tomorrow, can a citizen discover—quickly, simply, and without intimidation—*which* rule applied, *who* authored it, *when* it was approved, and *how* to challenge it?

Banking system impacts

On 10 March 2023, a queue began forming outside Silicon Valley Bank's branch in Santa Clara, California. By midday, depositors had attempted to withdraw more than $42 billion in a single day, according to the California Department of Financial Protection and Innovation's post-mortem. The physical line, long and anxious, lagged behind the digital stampede: most withdrawals began on phones. The lesson was uncomfortable but clear. When confidence shifts, liquidity moves at the speed of a thumb. That acceleration, visible in one vivid collapse, frames the central question of CBDC-era banking: what happens when the safest asset in the system—central bank money—sits a tap away?

The fear is straightforward. If retail users can convert deposits into CBDC instantly, deposit flight becomes less a panic than a precaution. A rumour, a misinterpreted earnings call, a viral screenshot of a balance-sheet footnote—any spark could trigger flows that dwarf past runs. Yet the countervailing insight is equally important. Policymakers do not have to choose between innovation and instability. Through design choices—tiers, caps, remuneration bands—CBDCs can support payments modernisation without hollowing out commercial banks.

Show the first major claim: liquidity is fragile. In March 2020, during the early pandemic shock, the Bank of England's weekly data showed a sharp rotation from risk assets into cash and near-cash instruments as firms and households sought security. Name the behaviour precisely. People moved into what they understood as the safest layer—central bank liabilities—either directly (banknotes) or indirectly (sight deposits guaranteed by the state). Explain the implication for CBDCs. If a digital form of that safest layer becomes frictionless, the queue outside a troubled bank is no longer a queue; it is a progress bar. The potential for rapid reintermediation must be anticipated, not feared.

The second major claim highlights the mitigation tools. The European Central Bank, in its July 2021 report, floated one option: a tiered remuneration model where small balances are remunerated neutrally while higher balances carry lower or even negative rates to discourage large-scale hoarding. Show this mechanism with numbers. If the neutral tier covered, say, €3,000 per user, customers could enjoy the convenience of CBDC for daily payments without shifting substantial savings. Larger deposits would remain with commercial banks, preserving their funding base. Explain why this matters. Banks lend against stable funding; a mass shift into CBDC would tighten credit, especially for small firms. Implication: remuneration bands become a quiet but decisive stability valve.

A second tool is transaction caps. The Bahamas' Sand Dollar, launched nationwide in October 2020, limits personal wallet balances to 8,000 BSD and restricts monthly transaction flows depending on the user's KYC level. Show how this plays out. Caps prevent the CBDC from becoming a wholesale funding substitute while still enabling everyday utility. Name the benefit. This design gives policymakers a predictable ceiling on liquidity migration. Explain the effect. Commercial banks retain their core deposits, which anchor lending. Implication: CBDC adoption scales without destabilising the institutions that support credit creation.

But safeguards must be tested against credible counter-cases. Consider Nigeria's eNaira, introduced in October 2021. Adoption remained low—research by the IMF (June 2023) estimated less than 2 per cent usage—yet the launch coincided with cash shortages during currency redesign efforts in early 2023. Amid frustration, some Nigerians speculated that the CBDC could be used to force digital-only behaviour. Even though this suspicion was not reflected in policy, the perception created resistance. The limitation here is trust. If users believe caps or tiers serve ulterior motives, safeguards morph into barriers. Reconciliation demands openness: publish remuneration schedules, publish cap rationales, and consult publicly before altering them. Predictability curbs suspicion.

Threaded through these examples is a motif: *the reservoir*. The banking system is a set of reservoirs—current accounts, savings accounts, money-market funds. CBDC adds a new reservoir. Its size, depth, and inflow controls determine whether a calm swap or a destabilising flood occurs.

The next claim centres on deposit competition. A CBDC could lure deposits away from banks in normal times if it offered superior convenience or perceived safety. Show the behaviour. A commuter in Manchester might shift her salary's first £500 into CBDC each month because it settles instantly across all merchants. A contractor in Bristol might keep a larger share of working capital in CBDC for predictable invoice clearing. Name the structural challenge. As small balances accumulate across millions of users, banks face marginally higher funding costs, especially if wholesale markets tighten. Explain the macro link. Higher funding costs translate into tighter lending conditions and reduced credit elasticity, particularly for SMEs. Implication: CBDCs must be framed as payment instruments, not savings instruments.

Regulators already have a template for balance control. Deposit insurance schemes—like the UK's FSCS—shape depositor behaviour by insuring up to £85,000 per institution. CBDCs could mirror this psychological threshold with similar soft limits: balances above a set level become non-remunerated or even constrained unless explicitly designated for specific purposes. Show how this works in practice. A household may keep £1,500 for day-to-day spending in CBDC but would hesitate to park £50,000 if remuneration were zero. Name the protective effect. Banks retain bulk deposits; CBDCs retain payment efficiency. Explain the design logic. Incentives, not mandates, align behaviour. Implication: stability emerges from calibrated friction.

Cross-border dynamics complicate the picture. If a CBDC is interoperable with foreign systems, capital could move rapidly during stress episodes. Show the risk. In a hypothetical UK–EU interoperable corridor, a rumour about a mid-sized lender in Leeds could lead to immediate flows into a euro CBDC. Name the precedent. During the 2010–12 eurozone crisis, households in Greece and Cyprus shifted deposits abroad through conventional banking channels; the flows were slower only because the rails were slower. Explain the CBDC-specific point. Instant settlement magnifies cross-border elasticity. Implication: safeguards must consider not only domestic reservoirs but foreign ones.

One counter-view deserves attention. Some economists argue that deposit flight is overstated because CBDCs will likely be non-interest-bearing in normal times, reducing their comparative appeal. Show the limitation. During shocks, people flee for safety, not yield. A non-interest-bearing CBDC could still attract flows if perceived as the safest asset. Reconcile the argument. Deposit flight is not constant; it is conditional. Safeguards can therefore be dynamic: remuneration bands tighten during stress, caps become temporarily firmer, and communication shifts to emphasise stability.

Transparency about these switches is essential. If a cap changes quietly, suspicion rises. If remuneration rates adjust without explanation, political backlash follows. The banking system is not merely a set of balance sheets; it is a confidence machine. And confidence is narrative-driven. During the 2008 crisis, the UK Treasury's swift public guarantees reassured depositors precisely because the guarantees were explicit, timed, and explained. A CBDC's safeguard adjustments must follow that pattern.

As the reservoir motif returns, its message sharpens. A system with an additional reservoir requires clear valves. And a citizen with an additional tap requires clarity on how fast that tap runs.

So the unresolved test is simple to phrase but hard to meet: can a CBDC be liquid enough to improve payments yet inelastic enough to preserve banking stability—and can citizens see, clearly and in advance, how the valves that govern this balance move?

Cross-border corridors

At 09:12 on 14 June 2022, the Bangko Sentral ng Pilipinas recorded the arrival of a remittance sent from Dubai only minutes earlier. A Filipino nurse working at Rashid Hospital had initiated the transfer during her break. The funds reached Manila almost instantly, arriving already converted into pesos at a mid-market rate. The bank noted the cost: under one US dollar. For her, the outcome was simple—her mother received money for groceries without waiting days or forfeiting a margin to opaque intermediaries. For policymakers, the moment was a live demonstration of a deeper point. When payment systems speak to one another directly, borders become technical constraints rather than economic choke points.

That single transaction sits at the edge of a larger transformation. Cross-border transfers, traditionally slow and costly, are being re-imagined as corridors—direct, rule-bound pathways between monetary systems. The corridor is a motif to hold on to. Its structure, width, and signposts determine whether value flows cleanly or becomes trapped in regulatory underbrush. CBDCs promise to widen these corridors and replace a patchwork of correspondent banks with programmable, interoperable channels. But widening a corridor also changes who can move through it, at what speed, and under whose law.

The first claim is that inefficiency today is not mysterious; it is engineered by the layers through which money must pass. Show the legacy mechanics. A worker in Johannesburg sending rand to a sibling in Lilongwe often triggers a chain: a local bank debits the sender, a correspondent in London or New York intermediates, and a Malawian bank finally credits the account. Name the behaviour that drives cost. Each intermediary charges a fee, demands compliance checks, and reconciles books at different times of day. Explain the CBDC contrast. If the South African Reserve Bank and the Reserve Bank of Malawi operated interoperable CBDC ledgers, the transfer could settle near-instantly in both currencies, with FX handled by an automated market maker pre-approved by both jurisdictions. Implication: capital moves with fewer hands touching it, lowering costs but raising questions about oversight.

FX—the engine of international payments—is the second hinge of this analysis. In the MAS–BIS "m-Bridge" pilot (Hong Kong, Thailand, UAE, China) in 2022, participating banks routed cross-border transactions in under thirty seconds using prototype CBDCs. Show what made this possible. FX conversion occurred within the corridor itself: banks posted buy and sell quotes directly into the platform. Name the structural shift. Conversion became a protocol-defined step rather than a separate marketplace. Explain the consequence. This reduces slippage and settlement risk, but it also relocates FX governance from market desks to shared infrastructure.

Implication: the corridor becomes both road and customs checkpoint.

A third claim centres on capital controls and policy autonomy. Some states rely on capital controls as stabilisers, particularly during stress episodes. Show the real behaviour. In 2015, Argentina's central bank enforced strict controls to preserve dollar reserves, limiting purchase volumes and requiring additional documentation for foreign transactions. Name the tension with CBDCs. If cross-border corridors permit instantaneous settlement, capital controls must operate at line speed. Explain the mechanism. Rules become executable code: a CBDC wallet querying a corridor gateway must be able to confirm eligibility, quota, and purpose instantaneously. Implication: the law becomes a predicate function. This preserves autonomy but only if the rule-set is published and contestable.

However, a counter-case tempers any linear story of efficiency. Consider India's UPI–Singapore PayNow link, operational from February 2023. Although the corridor works in seconds, adoption has required careful phase-ins, KYC alignment, and volume thresholds. Show the limitation. Even with compatible rails, differences in AML rules, user ID schemes, and complaint mechanisms constrain throughput. Reconcile the gap. Interoperability is not merely technical; it is institutional. True corridors require harmonised or at least interoperable legal interfaces.

Thread the corridor motif again: a corridor is only as safe as its gates. A CBDC system must define who opens them, how entries are logged, and what happens when a rule changes mid-flow.

The next claim concerns interoperability layers. Some central banks favour a hub-and-spoke model—each CBDC plugs into a shared interoperability hub governed by a consortium. Show its appeal. It mirrors the architecture of the SEPA clearing framework, launched in 2008 to harmonise euro payments. Name the benefit. Governance is distributed; no single state operates the hub unilaterally. Explain the trade-off. Performance depends on the hub's uptime and rule-setting body. Implication: sovereignty is pooled, not surrendered, but political will must maintain the pool.

Others prefer corridor-specific bridges. The Bank of England's 2022 discussion paper entertained scenarios where bilateral corridors would allow the digital pound to interoperate with selected partners under tailored FX and compliance rules. Show the shape of such a corridor. It is narrower but controlled. Name the strategic gain. Bilateral corridors can embed specific protections—such as caps for outbound flow during domestic stress—without negotiating multilateral consensus. Explain the limitation. Users may face varied experiences depending on destination, complicating adoption. Implication: a world of many corridors could mirror the pre-SWIFT fragmentation unless governance is coherent.

Bring the analysis down to the everyday user. A Kenyan teacher in Eldoret receives a remittance from Doha. Under a CBDC corridor, she sees the funds arrive with automatic shilling conversion, a timestamp, and a precise fee line. Show the visibility. She can audit the route: sending wallet → Qatari ledger → corridor gateway → Kenyan ledger. Name the significance. Her trust no longer depends on opaque correspondent networks. Explain the broader effect. Transparency empowers users but also governments, which can see flow patterns in real time. Implication: the corridor must embed privacy budgets, so visibility does not collapse into surveillance.

A deeper claim follows: interoperability reshapes competition. If CBDCs allow low-cost remittance providers to bypass card networks and correspondent banks, incumbents will face pressure to reduce margins. Show evidence. Between 2016 and 2022, fintech entrants such as Wise and Remitly helped cut average remittance costs on key UK corridors—from the UK to India, Kenya, and the Philippines—by several percentage points (World Bank Remittance Prices database, 2022). Name the competitive mechanism. Entrants exploited transparency and faster settlement to undercut bank spreads. Explain the CBDC angle. With programmable corridors, these efficiencies become structural rather than provider-specific. Implication: CBDCs may not dominate remittances, but they will set the cost floor.

Yet efficiency carries risks. A CBDC corridor with real-time FX poses new attack surfaces. Show a hypothetical. If a hostile actor floods a corridor with transactions designed to exploit timing mismatches in FX pricing, liquidity buffers could drain faster than traditional checks can respond. Name the governance gap. FX risk management, long embedded in private institutions, becomes partially algorithmic. Explain the design response. Corridors must include rate-limits, automated circuit breakers, and clear liability rules for FX posting. Implication: interoperability cannot outrun risk management.

Return to the corridor motif for the third time. A corridor can deliver goods or smuggle them; it can unite regions or concentrate power at its gates. Its blueprint determines which.

The final claim addresses fairness and predictability. If programmable corridors make targeted aid or subsidies cross-border, rules about residence, tax status, or eligibility must be transparent. Show a scenario. A dual-national living in Berlin receives a child benefit from the UK Treasury. The corridor must confirm residency, currency, and tax identifiers before settlement. Name the fairness question. If eligibility code is opaque or updated silently, recipients may face unexplained rejections. Explain the imperative. Corridors need versioned rule-sets, public consultation windows, and clear logs for contesting decisions. Implication: cross-border programmability amplifies domestic governance duties.

A counter-argument insists that too much transparency will slow innovation and reveal sensitive FX algorithms. Show the tension. FX desks protect proprietary pricing models; governments protect capital control triggers. Reconcile the debate. Transparency need not reveal algorithms—only policies. Code can be open to audit without exposing pricing strategy. Implication: accountability is compatible with discretion if boundaries are explicit.

The chapter's earlier themes—stability, fairness, and agency—converge here. A cross-border CBDC corridor is not only plumbing. It is a policy instrument, a diplomatic channel, and a user experience layered into one. Each design choice signals whose interests the corridor serves.

The unresolved question that closes the subchapter is deliberately simple and stubborn. If CBDC corridors can make remittances as fluid as messaging apps, can they also preserve the protections—capital safeguards, privacy rights, due process—that border regimes were designed to defend? Or will the widening of digital corridors demand a new constitutional vocabulary for money in motion?

Chapter 8
Decentralised and Cash-like Alternatives

Long before digital ledgers and consensus algorithms, resilience in money rested on an object so ordinary it felt beneath philosophical scrutiny: the banknote. Its power lay in its indifference. A note worked whether the lights were on or off, whether trust in institutions was rising or falling, and whether the user was wealthy, marginalised, or merely unlucky. That quiet universality—its refusal to interrogate the holder—made it one of the most extraordinary civic inventions of the modern age. Today, as states build programmable monetary rails, the question returns with unexpected force: what should stand alongside a CBDC to ensure that people retain agency when systems strain or authorities overreach?

The clue came in 2012, when supermarkets in Christchurch reopened after the earthquake using simple paper vouchers printed overnight by a local association. The official payments infrastructure lay fractured—ATMs offline, banks shuttered, telecoms intermittent. Yet groceries still moved, because the voucher, like cash, required no permission, no authentication server, and no settlement finality beyond a handshake. The episode is not nostalgia; it is a reminder that fragility in digital finance is rarely hypothetical. When complexity climbs, the value of instruments that bypass it grows. The world is building ever more elaborate monetary architecture, and yet the simplest rails, precisely because they are simple, remain indispensable.

That paradox—the march towards hyper-digitisation colliding with an enduring need for low-tech guarantees—frames the argument ahead. The chapter examines decentralised and cash-like systems not as ideological alternatives to sovereign money, but as necessary companions. Their shared purpose is to prevent any single rail from becoming a choke point. Whether through cryptographically collateralised stablecoins or paper vouchers redeemable during outages, these systems act as counterweights. They introduce diversity where monoculture would otherwise embed risk.

One theme threads through what follows: distribution of power. The appeal of decentralised instruments is not only their engineering trickery or their market liquidity, but their governance structure. Collateralised stablecoins cannot magic away risk, yet when their reserves are transparent, independently attested, and legally segregated, they create a discipline that public systems sometimes lack. The relationship is not adversarial. Well-designed market instruments can complement CBDCs by absorbing innovation risk, testing features in real time, and offering users hedges against operational failures. They can expose blind spots in official architectures: what happens when a state ledger pauses? Who keeps the economy moving during a software rollback? Sometimes the answer lies outside the state.

Privacy-preserving payment systems illustrate this again. Their promise is not secrecy but discretion: the ability to make small payments without those payments becoming entries in a behavioural dossier. Techniques like zero-knowledge proofs, blinded signatures, or payment codes are often framed as eccentric, confined to technologists or activists. That framing misses their civic potential. When implemented as public-interest tools—auditable, time-limited, and bounded by law—they become the digital analogue to handing over a fiver at a corner shop. Privacy by default is not an extremist impulse; it is the minimum standard for preventing monetary participation from becoming a data-extraction exercise.

The chapter then turns to physical and hybrid instruments—cash, vouchers, postal money orders—not as relics but as infrastructure. Their resilience is empirical. Cash keeps villages functioning during power cuts in Cumbria. Postal money orders bridge remittance gaps in rural India when digital systems falter. Disaster vouchers steady households after typhoons in the Philippines when telecom towers fall. These are not romantic exceptions; they are operational proofs that physical instruments underpin social continuity when digital channels choke. The question is not whether to preserve them, but how to integrate them meaningfully into a broader ecosystem.

Pluralism becomes the final destination. Interoperable public money does not mean a mandatory pivot into a single CBDC channel, but a network of rails able to substitute for one another. In telecoms, number portability broke monopoly power not by nationalisation or deregulation alone, but by guaranteeing that users could switch providers without losing identity. Monetary systems need an equivalent principle: the ability to move balances, identities, and guarantees across public and decentralised rails without punitive friction. Competition on rights, reliability, and transparency—rather than on opacity or inertia—becomes the discipline that protects citizens.

Here, the motif that opened the chapter reappears. The Christchurch voucher was valuable not because it challenged the state, but because it filled a gap the state could not, in that moment, close. Decentralised and cash-like systems are not replacements for public money. They are constitutional guardians: decentralising risk, distributing agency, and ensuring that failure in one part of the system does not force failure everywhere else.

The unresolved tension that leads the reader onward is this: as governments build programmable, tightly integrated digital currencies, will they cultivate the alternative rails that keep monetary freedom resilient? Or will the elegance of centralisation tempt them to let the quieter instruments wither, leaving society with fewer escape valves when the next strain arrives?

Stablecoins with constraints

At 2:17 p.m. on 15 November 2022, Circle Internet Financial froze 32 addresses holding roughly US$75,000 on the Ethereum network at the request of a United States law-enforcement agency. The action took seconds. The effect was instant. Wallets that had been able to settle payments moments earlier found themselves immobilised, their balances present yet unusable. The episode, recorded openly on-chain, exposed a reality often obscured by the rhetoric of decentralisation: even assets marketed as borderless and neutral can be governed with the precision of a surgical instrument when the issuer retains authority over redemption. The incident was neither scandal nor overreach; it was lawful compliance. Still, it demonstrated the structural truth at the heart of stablecoins: their stability is anchored not merely in collateral but in institutional governance that can intervene at any time. That duality—

programmable freedom, discretionary constraint—drives both their promise and their limits.

Stablecoins present a puzzle. They settle at machine speed and operate across jurisdictions without the friction of correspondent banking. Yet their credibility hinges on decidedly traditional disciplines: segregated reserves, audited statements, redemption at par. The paradox becomes sharper when these market instruments complement public rails rather than compete with them. When they are well-structured—transparent collateral, independent attestation, rule-bound intervention—they can expand the resilience and diversity of a monetary ecosystem precisely because they obey constraints that markets alone cannot supply.

The motif that recurs through this exploration is simple: *who guarantees what?* Every stablecoin answers this question differently, and the engineering of that answer determines its reliability far more than any technical flourish.

The first major claim rests on the character of collateral. Consider the transformation in Circle's monthly attestations from 2021 to late 2023, when the firm shifted nearly all reserves into short-dated U.S. Treasuries held via regulated money-market structures. Show the shift: a portfolio once dominated by commercial paper became one almost entirely backed by sovereign debt. Name the source: audits published by Grant Thornton (2023) documented the reallocation. Explain the reason: during market stress, commercial paper markets freeze; Treasury bills do not. The implication is direct. A stablecoin's par redemption becomes credible when the underlying reserve is both liquid and insulated from issuer discretion. Collateral is not a technical choice; it is an institutional commitment whose breaching would be publicly visible within hours.

A second example clarifies governance. In June 2020, the MakerDAO protocol experienced a dramatic collateral auction failure during the "Black Thursday" Ethereum price crash. The event unfolded as oracle updates lagged and liquidity evaporated; collateral auctions cleared at zero bids, creating millions in deficits. The protocol survived due to an emergency mint of MKR governance tokens to recapitalise the system. That decision—

software-mediated though it was—required a community vote, demonstrating that decentralised governance is neither mechanical nor emotionless. It is a political process encoded in contracts. The implication is unavoidable. Even systems claiming autonomy depend on human governance during crises. The real test is whether that governance is transparent, well-specified, and resistant to capture.

Yet there is a counter-example that tempers optimism. TerraUSD collapsed spectacularly in May 2022, wiping out more than US$40 billion in market value as its algorithmic stabilisation mechanism failed under pressure. No reserves, no redemptions, no circuit-breakers. Its crash served as a kind of stress test for the entire category. The failure did not prove that stablecoins are inherently fragile, but it demonstrated the boundary: without collateral, without enforceable claims, and without independent attestation, a stablecoin is a promise made of vapour. Reconciling the lesson is straightforward. The value of constrained stablecoins lies in their constraints—capital requirements, governance rules, and transparency obligations—not in claims of pure decentralisation.

The behaviour that users can see matters more than the abstractions that issuers proclaim. When a user redeems a unit at par within minutes, when reserve reports update monthly, when freeze lists and intervention rules are published in advance, trust becomes measurable as a sequence of visible decisions rather than a vague sentiment. Conversely, when documentation is sparse, audits irregular, or governance councils opaque, users behave accordingly: they diversify, reduce exposure, or exit altogether. Markets do not reward rhetoric; they reward verifiable discipline.

The interplay between market solutions and public rails emerges clearly when considering international corridors. Singapore's Monetary Authority, through its Project Orchid pilots (2022–2023), explored how private stablecoins might interoperate with a hypothetical retail CBDC. The experiment did not crown either model superior. Instead, it showed how private issuance could serve high-innovation environments—merchant integration, programmable coupons—while the public rail provided settlement finality and consumer protection. The implication is quiet but profound. A plural system can harness the strengths of both: the creativity and speed of private markets and the rule-bound guarantees of public institutions.

This complementarity becomes more significant when the public rail is under exceptional strain. A well-regulated stablecoin may provide redundancy during outages, enabling cross-border transfers or domestic payments when a CBDC ledger undergoes maintenance or rollback. It is not a replacement for sovereign money, but it can be a shock absorber. The image of a braided cord is useful here: each strand—CBDC, bank deposits, constrained stablecoins—shares load under tension, preventing the system from snapping when one strand alone would be overwhelmed.

Still, complementarity requires boundaries. Stablecoins without strict governance can distort policy transmission. If remuneration bands or holding limits apply to CBDCs but not to private stablecoins, users may shift balances en masse during policy shifts, undermining stabilisation goals. Public authorities therefore face a choice: either integrate stablecoins into the regulatory perimeter—capital rules, attestation schedules, redemption mandates—or risk a parallel monetary structure that ignores public aims. The decision is not ideological; it is operational. If stablecoins are to complement public rails, they must not erode the public's ability to govern monetary conditions.

Transparency becomes the hinge on which the relationship turns. A constrained stablecoin publishes not only reserve composition but redemption rules, intervention triggers, governance votes, and audit timelines. It gives users a ledger not just of balances but of rights. This is where some issuers succeed. Others fall short. The difference shows sharply in user behaviour: stablecoins with detailed attestations and predictable redemptions maintain their peg during stress; those with opaque structures wobble. Transparency is a risk-management mechanism, not a marketing device.

The recurring motif—*who guarantees what?*—returns at the end. A CBDC guarantees state-backed settlement finality. Bank deposits guarantee convertibility subject to prudential rules. Constrained stablecoins guarantee redemption at par backed by segregated reserves. Each instrument has a role. The friction arises when any one instrument assumes a monopoly. Markets innovate, sometimes recklessly; states stabilise, sometimes slowly. The healthiest monetary systems allow both impulses to coexist under clear guardrails.

The unresolved tension lies precisely there. As governments design CBDCs with powerful features and broad mandates, will they create space for tightly constrained, transparent stablecoins to operate as complementary rails? Or will regulatory pressure push them to the margins, reducing the system's diversity and leaving centralised infrastructure as the single point of resilience—and failure?

Privacy-preserving payments

At 10:03 a.m. on 8 June 2020, the Electric Coin Company published a technical bulletin detailing a vulnerability in the *Sprout* variant of Zcash. The flaw did not compromise user identities, but it allowed the construction of counterfeit notes undetectable by standard verification. The company disclosed the issue responsibly, patched it silently, and, crucially, revealed that no counterfeits had occurred. The episode unfolded with unusual transparency for a cryptographic project and revealed a truth often missed in policy debates: privacy-preserving payment systems do not live in shadows. They survive only if their mathematics and governance withstand public scrutiny. That paradox—opacity for the user, auditability for the system—is the tension that defines privacy technology when designed for the public good rather than the margins.

A second fact grounds the stakes. In 2019, the Financial Action Task Force (FATF) formalised its "travel rule" guidance, compelling financial institutions globally to attach identifying metadata to certain cross-border transfers above particular thresholds. The requirement aimed at traceability, not surveillance. Yet its broad scope immediately placed pressure on privacy-preserving tools. If a system could prove compliance without revealing identities, regulators would accept it. If it could not, it risked de facto exclusion. This moment, more than any ideological argument, demonstrated that privacy tools succeed not by hiding from law but by coexisting with it.

The recurring motif of this analysis—the question *who sees what?*—threads through every design choice in privacy-preserving payments. Systems that articulate this boundary clearly serve the public interest. Those that do not become niche curiosities or regulatory casualties.

The claim that privacy is a public good, not a fringe demand, requires showing its visible consequences. When a street vendor in Manila accepts QR payments through GCash, the buyer discloses phone data, transaction history, and metadata that can be correlated across providers. These disclosures accumulate, forming behavioural maps no individual intended to create. Name the research: the GSM Association's Mobile Money Report (2022) documented how merchant adoption surged in Southeast Asia while privacy controls lagged. Explain the mechanism: centralised wallets collect more data than is necessary for settlement because the economic incentives of platform providers favour profiling. The implication follows. Privacy-preserving payment techniques can counterbalance these incentives by design, limiting what even well-intentioned intermediaries can learn.

Zero-knowledge proofs (ZKPs) offer the clearest demonstration of this logic. They allow a user to prove a statement—"I am over 18"; "this transfer is below the threshold"; "the note is valid"—without revealing the underlying data. This is not magic; it is mathematics that converts a compliance requirement into a selective disclosure process. The best example sits not in cryptocurrency lore but in a regulated environment. The Swiss Federal Railways adopted zk-SNARKs in a 2018 trial to validate tickets without exposing travel itineraries. A guard could verify authenticity; the system learned nothing about origins or destinations. The principle is transferable to payments. If a CBDC or stablecoin rail allows a user to prove eligibility or legitimacy without revealing identity until legally required, privacy becomes a baseline rather than an optional mode.

Yet every technique has limits. Payment codes—used by systems such as BIP47 in Bitcoin—allow addresses to be derived undetectably, giving each counterparty a unique channel without repeated identity revelation. They prevent address reuse, a major vector of deanonymisation. But they also depend on out-of-band communication for the initial code exchange. In low-connectivity settings, this requirement becomes a friction. Reconciling the limitation demands acknowledging that privacy engineering is a portfolio, not a monolith. The strongest systems pair cryptographic proofs with communication primitives that respect human realities: unreliable networks, shared devices, and inconsistent literacy.

The abstraction of "privacy" becomes tangible when paired with behaviours users can see. When a wallet offers two buttons—"fast mode" and "private mode"—and the latter is hidden behind warnings or slower UX paths, most users will drift into the tracked mode through sheer convenience. Conversely, when the default is private, and selective disclosure appears only when required by law, users behave differently. They expect anonymity for small payments. They treat disclosures as exceptions rather than norms. They build patterns of behaviour that align with civic values rather than friction economics.

The first example of system-wide selective disclosure at scale comes from Belgium's eIDAS pilots in 2021–2022. Using anonymous credentials developed with the support of the KU Leuven COSIC group, citizens could authenticate age or residency without revealing full identity. The infrastructure proved that public-interest privacy could coexist with regulated services. More importantly, it showed a path for payments. If identifiers can be minimised for authentication, they can be minimised for settlement.

A credible counter-example comes from early implementations of "privacy coins" that relied on simple mixers. Mixers pool funds and redisperse them, but they require trust in operators and exhibit statistical leakage. The 2017 research by Möser, Böhme, and Breuker demonstrated that Bitcoin mixers leaked patterns sufficient for clustering, and subsequent law-enforcement operations exposed their fragility. This limitation does not undermine privacy-preserving payments; it distinguishes robust cryptography from superficial obfuscation. Reconciling the example reasserts the central theme: privacy works only when engineered as a public-interest utility, not a gimmick for evasion.

The implications of robust privacy extend beyond consumer protection. They shape political legitimacy. When citizens believe their small purchases, donations, or associations are visible to unknown observers, they self-censor. Behaviour changes before any formal rule is imposed. Privacy-preserving payment tools counter this chilling effect by restoring a space for unobserved lawful activity. The metric is not sentiment but usage: when private payment modes are easy, predictable, and default, adoption grows. When they are hidden or inconvenient, they gather dust.

The motif—*who sees what?*—reappears in settlement architecture. A system built on zero-knowledge proofs or payment codes can give auditors the visibility they require without granting operators unilateral insight into personal choices. The ledger records validity, not identity. Regulators receive aggregate compliance, not behavioural detail. Users retain autonomy. This is not perfect anonymity; it is structured privacy, governed by rules rather than the goodwill of institutions.

The unresolved tension sits exactly here. As states design CBDCs and update AML regimes, will they treat privacy-preserving techniques as civic infrastructure—worthy of investment, standardisation, and regulatory accommodation—or as curiosities best sidelined to avoid complexity? The decision will determine whether digital money inherits the dignity of cash or the surveillance risk of unchecked data platforms.

The question that follows—what must remain unseen, and by whom?—will decide whether privacy-preserving payments grow into tools of public purpose or remain confined to the margins, admired technically but distrusted politically.

Cash, vouchers, and postal rails

At 07:42 on 5 March 2011, in Ishinomaki on Japan's Miyagi coast, postal officers began handing out the first paper *fukkō* vouchers to residents displaced by the Tōhoku earthquake and tsunami. Banks were shut, telecom towers were down, and ATMs lay flooded under metres of seawater. Yet within hours, families could buy fuel, food, and medicine using stamped slips redeemable offline by any participating merchant. The Ministry of Internal Affairs and

Communications later reported that over ¥37 billion worth of these vouchers circulated in the region during the first month alone (MIC, 2011). The system's success rested on three visible properties: it worked without connectivity, it required no specialised device, and it drew on institutional trust earned long before the disaster. These slips, printed at speed, did what sophisticated digital wallets could not. They moved value when nothing else moved.

The episode revealed a paradox that still unsettles digital designers. Why do fragile, low-tech instruments outperform advanced payment systems when conditions deteriorate? The answer sits in their failure modes. Cash and vouchers degrade gracefully. Networks do not. And when the question becomes survival rather than convenience, graceful degradation beats efficiency every time.

This motif—*what survives the outage?*—anchors the argument for physical and hybrid payment rails. It is not nostalgia. It is operational realism.

The first claim requires a scene. In late October 2012, when Hurricane Sandy hit New York, lower Manhattan lost power for days. Card terminals died. Mobile networks sagged. The Federal Reserve Bank of New York recorded a surge in cash withdrawals in the preceding 48 hours, followed by reliance on neighbour-to-neighbour lending once machines went dark. Show the behaviour: residents queued at the few functioning ATMs, then used physical notes for everything from petrol rations to makeshift childcare payments. Name the event: FRBNY's 2013 "Operational Risk Review" documented the breakdown. Explain its significance: when settlement systems fail, people revert to instruments they can verify with their eyes and hands. The implication is unavoidable. Any national payment architecture that lacks cash-like resilience becomes brittle precisely when society most needs steadiness.

A second example demonstrates hybrid adaptability. After the 2010 Haiti earthquake, the Red Cross and Mercy Corps distributed paper vouchers redeemable at local markets. These vouchers bore serial numbers, expiry dates, and holograms but required no electricity. The UN Office for the Coordination of Humanitarian Affairs (OCHA) recorded that 96 per cent of participating households used them for essentials in the first distribution cycle. Show the mechanism: a merchant accepted a voucher, marked it redeemed, and later exchanged it with an NGO for cash or credit, often through postal networks. Explain the economics: the system preserved dignity and choice, avoided centralised queues, and encouraged market recovery. The implication extends beyond disaster response. Even in functioning economies, hybrid instruments—paper vouchers, prepaid cards with offline limits, postal money orders—serve as buffers that keep economic activity flowing when the dominant digital rail stutters.

Yet a credible counter-example must be addressed. During India's November 2016 *demonetisation*, the withdrawal of high-denomination notes caused severe disruption. Physical cash, once the resilience layer, became scarce overnight. The limitation is clear. Physical rails only protect the public if authorities maintain predictability and continuity. When supply is suddenly restricted, the very instrument meant to provide stability becomes a source of instability. Reconciling the case requires reasserting the motif. What survives the outage is not cash per se but the guarantee that its supply will not be weaponised or withdrawn without due preparation. Physical instruments need governance as much as digital ones.

The next claim concerns vouchers and postal rails as complements to digital money, not competitors. Consider the United Kingdom's Post Office Horizon system, which—despite the scandal surrounding its accounting software—illustrates a deeper point about physical reach. The Post Office provides cash access to millions who live beyond reliable broadband or who prefer not to operate digital wallets. Behavioural studies commissioned by the FCA in 2021 noted that older adults termed the Post Office "the last dependable branch," precisely because its services remain tangible. Show the behaviour: a person withdraws £40, hands it to a tradesperson, and both leave with the settlement complete. No battery, no server, no latency. Explain the structure: postal rails serve as a physical interface to the state's monetary system. The implication for a digital era is subtle. Even the most advanced CBDC must coexist with institutions capable of mediating offline value transfers at scale.

The hybridity emerging in global pilots reflects this lesson. In China's e-CNY trials (2020–2023), hardware wallets with secure elements enabled offline person-to-person transfers for small values. Users tapped devices together, executing a transfer that settled locally and synchronised once connectivity returned. Manufacturers such as PAX and Ingenico produced point-of-sale terminals capable of accepting both e-CNY and conventional cash, creating a bridge between digital rails and established merchant routines. Show the behaviour: a fruit vendor in Suzhou accepts an offline e-CNY payment during a temporary network outage. Name the mechanism: dual-chip security modules. Explain its virtue: the system never collapses to zero. The implication for liberal democracies is clarifying. Offline-first design is not exotic. It is simply the digital articulation of what cash already provides.

The second named example sits in Europe. In 2022, the Banque de France tested offline CBDC settlement using prepaid QR vouchers distributed through participating retailers in Aix-en-Provence. These vouchers allowed citizens to transact without mobile coverage, with redemption occurring through settlement agents days later. The pilot's technical report emphasised that offline vouchers served as a cap on systemic risk: they limited value, constrained fraud exposure, and continued functioning during grid instability. The behaviour visible to users—scan, check, hand over—mirrored cash. The implication is profound. Hybrid rails succeed when they feel natural, not novel.

The careful pairing of abstractions with behaviours deepens the argument. "Resilience" becomes a merchant handing over a QR voucher during a blackout. "Inclusivity" becomes a pensioner using a postal money order because mobile data is too costly. "Continuity" becomes a local council distributing printed fuel credits during a snowstorm when digital portals freeze. These behaviours reveal why physical instruments endure: they compress institutional trust into artefacts that remain usable when infrastructure collapses.

Nevertheless, physical rails carry costs. They require secure printing, distribution logistics, and controls against counterfeiting. They lack granular programmability, limiting targeted relief. And they constrain real-time oversight, which regulators may view as a drawback. But the limitation is reconcilable. Not every payment rail must optimise for the same properties. CBDCs excel at auditability. Vouchers excel at failover. Postal money orders excel at geographic reach. A resilient national architecture blends these strengths rather than forcing convergence on a single paradigm.

Threading the motif again—*what survives the outage?*—invites a sharper question. How should states design hybrid rails that remain trustworthy without becoming ungovernable? The answer lies in boundary-setting. Digital instruments should inherit cash's anonymity for low-value payments. Physical vouchers should expire predictably and transparently. Postal rails should maintain service guarantees backed by statute. CBDC wallets should recognise voucher and cash inputs without penalising the user. These boundaries ensure complementarity rather than erosion.

A final implication demands attention. Hybrid instruments become crucial not only in disasters but also in contested civic moments. When trust in digital infrastructure drops—whether due to outages, misconfigurations, or political anxiety—citizens turn to physical value. Systems that honour this instinct strengthen legitimacy. Systems that penalise it weaken the social contract.

The question that remains—how much physical capacity a digital-first economy must preserve—is unresolved. The answer will define whether resilience becomes a ceremonial afterthought or a living guarantee.

Interoperable public money

On 1 February 2014, when the Single Euro Payments Area (SEPA) migration deadline arrived across the European Union, a curious sight emerged in Frankfurt's financial district. Small firms, long dependent on domestic transfers, found themselves making cross-border payments as casually as sending an email. Deutsche Bundesbank officers later noted that the cutover, though uneven, produced an immediate reduction in processing frictions for routine payments (Bundesbank, 2015). A florist in Offenbach could settle an invoice in Lyon with the same data fields, the same settlement window, and—crucially—the same consumer protections. The uniformity felt almost physical, like rails laid to a common gauge. What mattered was not that one system won, but that many systems could speak to each other.

This early demonstration of monetary interoperability frames a wider paradox. Why, in a century defined by digital abundance, do payment systems still behave like islands? And what does it mean for a state contemplating a central bank digital currency to insist that it become *only* one island among many? The tension between sovereignty and pluralism sits at the centre of this debate. It forces a question that recurs throughout this book: *How do we build systems that protect people not by concentrating power but by distributing it?*

That motif—rails that remain plural—threads through this subchapter. Every architecture gains strength from its junctions, not its walls.

The first claim requires a tangible scene. In Brazil, the launch of Pix in November 2020 transformed retail payments almost overnight. The Banco Central do Brasil required participating banks, payment institutions, and wallets to expose common APIs. Show the behaviour: a street vendor in São Paulo receives instant payment from a customer using a wallet issued by a different provider. Name the mechanism: Pix's open participant model, which mandated technical conformity rather than corporate homogeneity. Explain its significance: interoperability lowered switching costs for users, who could abandon a poor-quality provider without losing access to the rail. The implication is decisive for CBDC design. A public rail gains legitimacy when it supports exits, not when it traps users.

A second example demonstrates the civic dimension of open rails. India's Unified Payments Interface (UPI), launched in April 2016, required each bank and wallet to interoperate through the NPCI's shared interface. Show the behaviour: a worker in Jaipur sends wages to a relative in Kochi using a UPI ID, regardless of which banks or apps either party uses. Name the mechanism: the NPCI's mandate that all participants support push–pull payments over the same addressing scheme. Explain the virtue: interoperability creates functional competition on latency, interface quality, and reliability, rather than on exclusive networks. The implication for CBDCs is subtle but powerful. A state digital currency should amplify competition, not mute it.

A credible counter-example clarifies the boundary. Kenya's M-Pesa, launched in 2007, achieved extraordinary inclusion but long resisted interoperability with rival mobile money platforms. Users often resorted to costly withdrawal–deposit hops to move value across ecosystems. The limitation is clear: dominance without competition locks users into suboptimal service. Yet reconciling the case illuminates our motif once more. M-Pesa succeeded despite its closed rail because the alternative was banking exclusion. But as digital maturity grows, closed rails become less defensible. Interoperability evolves from luxury to expectation.

The next claim concerns the role of CBDC as *one* public rail among several, not the master rail. This distinction is not rhetorical. Consider the United Kingdom's Faster Payments Service (2008), which enabled near-instant domestic transfers long before any retail CBDC pilot. FPS coexists with CHAPS for high-value settlement, with card networks for point-of-sale transactions, and with cash for offline use. Show the behaviour: a small business pays suppliers by FPS, accepts card payments from customers, and retains a petty-cash box for contingencies. Name the interaction: multi-rail liquidity management. Explain the structure: different rails serve different tolerances—speed, cost, reliability, offline utility. The implication for CBDC design is straightforward. A CBDC should enrich the ecosystem, not homogenise it.

Pluralism also shapes how rights are secured. A single dominant rail risks becoming the "choke point" through which policy errors, outages, or overreach propagate at scale. Multiple interoperable rails dilute this risk. They create contestability—a user can walk away. That behavioural freedom reinforces institutional restraint. If a CBDC wallet imposes new frictions, users shift to stablecoins, vouchers, or bank deposits. This is not a threat to public money. It is insurance for its legitimacy.

The next claim requires we pair abstractions with behaviours. "Fairness" becomes a migrant worker in Milan choosing a low-fee remittance provider without sacrificing regulatory protections. "Transparency" becomes a wallet displaying its supported rails, limits, and privacy guarantees in unambiguous text. "Reliability" becomes a user switching providers after repeated service outages, with no disruption to their addressing scheme. Each behaviour evidences the same principle: rights become real when exit becomes simple.

Consider cross-border corridors. The Bank for International Settlements, through its Project Dunbar (2022), tested multi-CBDC platforms enabling direct cross-border settlement between Australia, Malaysia, Singapore, and South Africa. Show the behaviour: a corporate treasurer in Kuala Lumpur settles an invoice in Australian dollars without routing through multiple correspondent banks. Name the mechanism: a shared settlement layer governed by participating central banks. Explain the significance: such corridors demonstrate how sovereign monies can interoperate without ceding monetary autonomy. The implication is that CBDCs need not become monolithic. They can be modular components of a broader public-money mesh.

A second cross-border example underscores the user-facing gains. During the ECB–Bank of Canada 2019 experiments using distributed ledgers for international payments, participants observed that harmonised messaging formats reduced reconciliation delays. Show the behaviour: a firm in Montréal receives euro-settled proceeds within minutes instead of days. Name the mechanism: synchronisation protocols using standardised data models. Explain the benefit: friction reduction arises not from replacing each rail but from making them speak clearly to one another. The implication is architectural rather than ideological. Interoperability is a discipline.

Yet interoperability alone does not eliminate power imbalances. A credible limitation appears when dominant platforms leverage their scale to shape user behaviour. If a large wallet provider defaults to its proprietary rail for revenue reasons—even when a public rail is cheaper—interoperability exists in theory but not in practice. Reconciling the limitation requires guardrails: mandated support for all approved public rails, explicit opt-in for proprietary ones, and user-facing clarity on fees and privacy. Without such guardrails, pluralism becomes a slogan.

Thread the motif again: rails that remain plural. The image invites a wider reflection on sovereignty. Monetary sovereignty is not undermined by competition; it is strengthened by it. A CBDC that coexists with bank deposits, regulated stablecoins, vouchers, and postal or offline instruments becomes one pillar in a resilient structure. Users choose based on rights, reliability, and convenience. Providers earn trust. Public money earns legitimacy.

The final claim concerns the governance of interoperability. Standards must be open. APIs must be published. Reference wallets must exist to test compliance. Dispute mechanisms must operate across rails. These design choices sound technical, but their consequences are constitutional. They determine whether a user is free to move value without penalty or permission beyond what the law requires. Show the behaviour: a parent switches from a commercial wallet to a public reference wallet to exercise stricter privacy controls, with their address and transaction history intact. Name the mechanism: data portability backed by statute. Explain the virtue: mobility disciplines power. The implication is that interoperability is not merely an engineering goal. It is a democratic one.

All of this returns us to the question that opened the subchapter. Why do payment systems behave like islands? Because building bridges requires intentional design—and intentional humility. A CBDC that assumes primacy will function, but it will not flourish. A CBDC that embraces pluralism, supports exits, and competes on rights and reliability will evolve into a public instrument worthy of its mandate.

The unresolved tension remains deliberately open. How many bridges must a sovereign build for citizens to feel free—and how many islands can it tolerate before fragmentation erodes cohesion?

Chapter 9
What Good Looks Like: Design Principles

At 11:42 on 9 August 2019, Singapore's national digital identity service faltered for the second time that week. The outage lasted only minutes, yet it froze access to banking portals, halted tax submissions, and trapped thousands of residents in a quiet, unplanned standstill. When the incident report appeared months later, its most unsettling detail was not the technical fault itself but the revelation that several subsystems had retained more diagnostic data than strictly necessary. A flaw multiplied by unnecessary records became a moment of national vulnerability. The lesson was simple. Systems meant to empower citizens must be built on an ethic of minimalism: hold as little as possible, for as short as possible, and be able to prove the deletion.

The paradox sharpened that year in a very different setting. During a power outage in rural Hokkaido, a chain of small shops continued trading using pre-printed vouchers pegged to a fixed yen value, redeemable when connectivity returned. The improvised system worked because it trusted modest transactions to humanity rather than machinery. It leaned on a principle older than electricity: small value, low risk, and mutual responsibility. In their own way, those handwritten chits offered a miniature blueprint for resilient digital money. Where a system places its thresholds—and how it behaves when they are breached—reveals its political character as much as its technical one.

This chapter begins in those moments of stress because they show what design principles are *for.* They are not ornaments or slogans but the guardrails that determine whether digital money behaves as a servant or a master. A payment system without strict data minimisation invites mission creep. A wallet whose functions cannot be explained in plain language invites manipulation. An architecture that collapses in an outage betrays its users at the very moment they need it most. And a system shielded from public testing invites the slow rot of complacency. Principles become the backbone of citizenship in a digital monetary age.

The opening principle—least authority, least data—demands intellectual precision. It is the opposite of the data maximalism that defined early platform capitalism. Least authority asks whether each subsystem truly needs its privileges, and what harm could arise if those privileges are abused. Least data interrogates retention: if a system stores timestamps by default, are they pruned? If deletion is promised, can it be audited? This principle is architectural and moral. It forces designers and policymakers to articulate what they must not know. That restraint becomes the floor on which trust can stand.

From here, the chapter pivots to explainability and consent, taking them as practical duties, not aspirational virtues. A citizen should be able to inspect the functions that move their money—inspection in the broadest sense, whether by reading a plain-language explanation, verifying source code, or cross-examining a civil-society report. Consent must not be a labyrinth of grey buttons and coercive defaults. It must be legible and reversible. A power exercised in secret ceases to be a power granted by the public; it becomes a power taken. The shift from promise to clarity is the dividing line between a democratic rail and a paternalistic one.

The chapter then moves to the principle of *fail-open* behaviour for small payments. Fail-open is a phrase that sounds technical, but its meaning is social: low-value payments must continue even when the wider system buckles. Cash performs this task effortlessly. A digital architecture must work harder. It must guarantee that outages do not silence the poor before they inconvenience the powerful. It must retain space for small, anonymous exchanges that maintain dignity and autonomy when networks are down. Fail-open design interrupts the temptation to criminalise ordinary life in the name of risk management.

Finally, the chapter builds towards sunlight and stress tests. In aviation, in public health, and in cybersecurity, drills and disclosures are the crucible of resilience. What survives scrutiny tends to serve the public. What avoids scrutiny tends to serve itself. Public drills test not only the machinery but the governance; they reveal whether an institution welcomes accountability or fears it. Independent adversarial testing—performed by those who have no stake in protecting reputations—offers a clearer window into systemic strength than any glossy launch briefing. The stress test becomes a democratic ritual: a probationary moment in which the system must earn the public's trust.

Across these themes sits a quiet motif: the difference between power requested and power granted. Every design principle marks the boundary. Least authority defines what government is allowed to reach. Explainability defines what citizens can understand and challenge. Fail-open defines what remains in their hands when the machinery falters. Sunlight defines how well institutions tolerate scrutiny. Together they form a kind of unwritten constitution for digital money—a constitution not of parchment but of practice.

As this chapter unfolds, it will return to that motif again and again. You will see how minimalism strengthens security rather than weakens it; how clarity protects consent; how small, anonymous payments safeguard the social contract; how public testing disciplines institutions that might otherwise drift. The deeper argument running beneath each section is that design principles are not constraints on innovation but the terms through which innovation earns legitimacy.

What, then, counts as "good" in a monetary system that increasingly blends code, law, and civic expectation? And how should a nation decide which principles deserve to be non-negotiable? The pages ahead do not settle those questions. They sharpen them. They invite you to examine the scaffolding beneath the systems we already use—and the systems we may soon inherit—and to ask which principles ensure that power flows outward to citizens rather than inward to institutions.

Least authority, least data

At 14:03 on 25 May 2018, the Irish Data Protection Commission published its first post-GDPR enforcement notice. The target was a regional health authority in Cork that had stored patient records—

including diagnostic notes and medication histories—far longer than required. The revelation was banal and alarming at once. No malicious actor had breached the system; nothing dramatic had occurred. The harm lay in the quiet accumulation of data that no longer served its purpose. Retention drift had turned routine administration into latent exposure. Cork became a case study not because it was unusual, but because it was typical. Systems that collect data tend to keep it. Systems that keep data tend to spread it. And once spread, it resists deletion.

The paradox deepened a year later when Berlin's transport operator, BVG, admitted that its e-ticketing logs—intended to support fraud detection—had been retained for months, not days. The logs mapped daily commutes, medical trips, and patterns of religious observance. The agency corrected the process within weeks, but the episode exposed a deeper truth: governance failures thrive in the shadows of operational convenience. BVG had not set out to track its citizens. It had merely allowed lax retention to calcify. When the German Federal Commissioner for Data Protection reviewed the case in 2019, his public statement captured the dilemma: data minimisation is not a philosophical ideal; it is a risk boundary.

If digital money is to maintain public legitimacy, this boundary must become non-negotiable. The architecture must commit to *least authority, least data* as a foundational promise. Authority should be sliced as thinly as possible; data should evaporate as soon as its task is complete. And deletion must be more than a claim. It must be auditable, testable, and provable by those outside the system. Only then does the burden of proof shift where it belongs: away from citizens defending their privacy, and towards institutions demonstrating their restraint.

The motif that threads through this discussion is simple: *what is not collected cannot be abused.* It appears in different forms—Cork's overgrown records, Berlin's overstretched logs—but the core lesson stays steady. Data that persists beyond purpose becomes a liability. Power that exceeds necessity becomes a threat.

The first major claim rests on a practical demonstration. When the Bank of Canada launched its Project Jasper Phase III trial in Toronto in 2017, engineers showed how selective disclosure could support wholesale settlement without exposing underlying transaction data. They named the technique explicitly: zero-knowledge range proofs, adapted to validate value bounds without revealing counterparties. Their approach explained something critical: constraints built into the system reduce the need for privileged access. The implication was larger than the experiment. If the architecture can prove correctness without opening the ledger, supervisory authority can shrink. Least authority becomes an engineering choice, not an aspiration.

The second example comes from the Netherlands, where the Dutch Payments Association in 2020 piloted a protocol for automatic deletion of low-risk transaction metadata used for fraud scoring. The protocol defined a timer: ninety minutes. If no anomaly was detected within that window, the ephemeral scoring data vanished. This concrete behaviour—scheduled deletion tied to operational need—made the abstraction of data minimisation visible. It measurable reduced exposure. And it forced planners to articulate *why* any new data should persist longer. Least data became a discipline, not a slogan.

But no principle survives without encountering a counter-example. The United Kingdom's Financial Conduct Authority, after a series of AML reviews in 2021, argued that prolonged retention of certain high-risk transaction logs was essential to support complex investigations. The FCA position appeared to clash with minimisation. Yet when pressed by the Information Commissioner's Office later that year, the limitation emerged: the agency could justify retention only if it implemented tiered access, strong warrant thresholds, and cryptographic controls that ensured investigators saw only what they were authorised to see. The reconciliation came through design: long retention without granular authority is a privacy failure; precise authority without justified retention is an evidentiary failure. Least authority and least data meet in the middle by forcing institutions to defend both duration and privilege.

These examples anchor a broader claim: abstractions such as *trust* or *efficiency* gain meaning only when tied to observable choices. A system that deletes payment timestamps after twenty-four hours signals trustworthiness. A wallet that prompts users before expanding permission scopes demonstrates respect for autonomy. A central bank that publishes deletion audit logs—signed, timestamped, and independently verifiable—converts efficiency claims into measurable outcomes. If deletion cannot be proved, it cannot be trusted.

The motif returns: *what is not collected cannot be abused.* To embed that ethic within a CBDC, least authority must be applied at every layer. At the device level, the wallet should process routine risk checks locally. At the protocol level, validation should occur without revealing identifiers unless strictly required. At the institutional level, each privileged action—data access, rule invocation, compliance review—must leave a signed, public trace. Authority becomes something that can be counted rather than assumed.

To show how this principle shapes behaviour, consider the dynamics of governance drift. In Estonia's ID system in 2017, after a vulnerability in its national smart cards became public, auditors discovered that temporary risk-assessment logs had been retained for far longer than intended. The discovery forced the government to implement formal deletion ceremonies—cryptographically signed events proving that specified data had been destroyed. That visible ritual changed institutional behaviour. It imposed friction; it demanded justification. Minimisation moved from the margins of policy to the centre of operations.

A similar lesson emerged in South Korea during the 2020 COVID-19 contact-tracing rollout. The government collected location logs from telecoms and credit card companies. Although the programme was lawful and time-limited, civil society groups demanded—and eventually secured—a commitment to public deletion audits. The Ministry of Health published verification reports showing when and how batches of data had been purged. These reports, combined with sunset clauses, helped maintain democratic consent in a period of exceptional state authority. The implication for digital currencies is stark: extraordinary powers must be constrained by extraordinary transparency.

At this point, a reasonable critic may ask whether strict minimisation reduces investigative capability or operational insight. The limitation is real. Certain analyses benefit from longitudinal data. But minimisation does not mandate blindness. It requires proportion. Rather than raw histories, systems can retain aggregates. Rather than identifiers, they can store hashes. Rather than perpetual logs, they can keep rolling windows. The engineering palette is wide. The difficulty lies not in the technology but in the discipline of restraint. Absent that discipline, minimisation collapses into aspiration.

Least authority, too, faces tension. Oversight bodies often argue they require expansive privileges to perform their duties. Yet history shows the danger. The NSA's bulk telephony metadata program, revealed in 2013, accumulated records far beyond investigative necessity. The US Privacy and Civil Liberties Oversight Board later determined it had produced minimal intelligence value. Retrospective deletion was impossible; the data had reproduced itself across systems. Least authority would have prevented the expansion in the first place. Least data would have limited the footprint. And the absence of both principles became a lesson written in institutional regret.

The CBDC context magnifies these lessons. Monetary data is intimate. It maps relationships, priorities, and vulnerabilities. It sketches a life. The architecture must treat that intimacy as sacred. It must default to the minimum: the minimum data to settle a transaction, the minimum metadata to maintain integrity, the minimum authority to administer the rail. Every extra field, every extended retention period, every privileged API call must be justified in writing and tested in daylight.

Deletion sits at the centre of this ethic. A claim of deletion is insufficient. Deletion must be auditable. That requires cryptographic proof, not managerial assurance. Techniques such as verifiable erasure certificates or Merkle-tree-based deletion attestations can show that data was not only removed but cannot be resurrected by an insider. Independent monitors—civil society, academics, external auditors—must be able to validate the deletion events themselves. In this model, deletion becomes an act of governance, not of discretion.

The motif strikes again: *what is not collected cannot be abused.* When deletion is real, when authority is lean, the system does not need to rely on trust in personalities. It relies on verifiable behaviour. And verifiable behaviour lasts longer than promises.

At the heart of the subchapter sits one question that cannot yet be resolved: how much data, for how long, with what guardrails? The boundary will shift as policies evolve. The danger is that the shift becomes one-way. Minimisation restrains that drift. It forces policymakers to choose narrow tools over broad ones and to articulate why their choices deserve public consent.

The reader is therefore left with a tension: what should be the default when the convenience of retention competes with the dignity of deletion? And who should decide when that balance tilts too far?

Explainability and consent

At 09:12 on 21 July 2021, Luca Zanettin, a lawyer in Padua, opened Italy's official Immuni contact-tracing app and discovered that a silent update had changed how proximity scores were calculated. The update did not alter the law. It did not request new permissions. Yet it shifted citizens' exposure risk overnight. Only after journalists pressed the Ministry of Health did a plain-language explanation appear, revealing that an algorithmic threshold had been tightened to reduce false negatives. The intention was defensible. The manner was not. A rule that affected millions had been edited without being legible to them. Consent had been presumed because it was convenient. Agency dissolved into obscurity.

A similar lesson emerged in Oslo in May 2020 when the Norwegian Data Protection Authority ruled that the Smittestopp app must be suspended. The problem was not merely its continuous GPS logging; it was the opacity of the system's design. Users could not know what the app recorded, when it transmitted, or how long the data lived. Consent became fictional. The Authority's condemnation was precise: features that cannot be explained cannot be consented to. The suspension showed the cost of opacity. Trust evaporated because understanding was impossible.

For digital money, where rules can be encoded, updated, and enforced at machine speed, explainability becomes constitutional. Consent is not a one-time gesture but a continuous right. The wallet is not a form; it is a contract. And that contract must be readable, testable, and contestable by more than engineers. It must be visible to civil society, journalists, and ordinary citizens who wish to understand how their money behaves.

A quiet motif repeats throughout this subchapter: *nothing about us without clarity*. It appears in Padua's surprise update, Oslo's opaque logging, and the broader question of whether citizens can meaningfully understand the systems that govern their transactions.

The first major claim requires a demonstration drawn from payments rather than health data. When the European Central Bank released its prototype documentation for the digital euro in September 2022, it included a public specification for offline validation rules. The document named each constraint explicitly: value caps, counter increment limits, and the precise conditions under which the wallet must re-sync with the network. By publishing a human-readable model, the ECB explained the logic behind the wallet's behaviour. The implication was clear: transparency reduces reliance on institutional assurances. A rule that can be read and tested becomes a rule that can be trusted.

The second example comes from Singapore. In 2021, the Monetary Authority of Singapore (MAS) began requiring consumer-facing fintechs to publish change logs that distinguished between functional updates, data-access expansions, and risk-related modifications. This visible behaviour—separating categories and explaining them—transformed abstractions like *consent* into concrete steps. The logs were short, precise, and written in plain English. Civil society groups such as the Association of Women for Action and Research could examine them without specialist training. Consent became something a citizen could *measure* rather than something they were expected to imagine.

Limitations, however, must be faced. Japan's FSA argued in a 2022 consultation that publishing granular change logs could expose attack surfaces or reveal sensitive operational details. Their concern was not trivial. Over-disclosure can undermine security. The reconciliation came through segmentation. High-level behaviour changes could be published in plain language, while low-level code movements remained internal. The principle survived by differentiating transparency of effect from transparency of implementation. Citizens need to understand what changes for them. They do not need to read the cryptographic libraries.

Explainability therefore depends on design discipline. A wallet that rewrites its permissions without prompting signals a governance failure. A wallet that issues a clear, reversible consent request—time-stamped, logged locally, and visible to independent auditors—shows respect for user agency. And a wallet that allows civil society to replicate its logic in test harnesses transforms explainability into a communal right rather than a corporate privilege.

To illustrate this, consider the behaviour of South Africa's National Credit Regulator in 2019 when it discovered that several digital lenders were embedding pre-ticked consent boxes in their mobile interfaces. Users were enrolling in data-sharing schemes unintentionally. After public pressure, the Regulator mandated explicit consent prompts with no default options. The change produced a measurable shift: opt-in rates fell sharply, exposing the scale of accidental consent. The normative lesson extends to digital currencies. If consent is easy to give but hard to revoke, it is not consent. If prompts are designed to steer users into tracked modes, the system is exercising power, not offering choice.

The motif returns: *nothing about us without clarity*. This is not a slogan but an operational rule. Clarity must be enacted through architecture. For a CBDC wallet, this means that features—tax incentives, transaction caps, parental controls, accessibility settings—must be documented in forms that ordinary people can understand. If a spending limit is introduced, the user must see its value, duration, and rationale. If a new compliance routine is added, the event must appear in a public change log. The behaviour must be testable: civil society must be able to run a transaction through a reference wallet and see the rule activated exactly as described.

But explanation alone is insufficient. Contestability is the second half of the principle. A rule that cannot be challenged is a rule that can quietly expand. In 2016, the UK Investigatory Powers Tribunal issued a landmark judgment after privacy groups challenged secret bulk interception warrants. The Tribunal found that many safeguards had not been sufficiently disclosed, and it forced the government to rewrite its public guidance. The case showed how contestability keeps power aligned with law. The implication for digital money is direct: explainability must come with mechanisms that allow civil society to contest unclear or excessive features.

The counter-example helps clarify this boundary. China's rollout of the digital yuan through pilot cities such as Shenzhen and Suzhou between 2020 and 2022 included several operational updates that altered wallet telemetry. Although the system complied with Chinese domestic law, details were not consistently published. The absence of transparent change logs meant independent researchers had limited visibility into what changed and why. The limitation is not whether the system met policy aims; it is whether citizens had a meaningful way to understand and challenge new behaviours. The contrast reveals the cost of opacity in environments where feedback loops are narrow.

Explainability does not require technical simplicity. It requires communicative discipline. Complex systems can still be legible. Consider the UK's GOV.UK design guidelines introduced in 2012, which mandated plain-language explanations for every public-facing feature. The guidelines became a model for clarity because they assumed something radical: that complexity should never be the citizen's burden. Applied to digital money, the same principle means that a wallet must present its rules in language that a teenager, a pensioner, or a foreign resident can understand. Complexity belongs behind the curtain; comprehension belongs in the user's hand.

Consent, too, must be subject to the same ethic. It must be reversible. It must be quick. It must be logged. A system that remembers every acceptance but never records revocation creates an asymmetry of power. The Danish Data Protection Authority's decision in February 2022 against a financial app that made revocation practically impossible illustrates the point. Users could sign up in one tap but could withdraw only through a multi-step email process. The Authority judged the design coercive. For CBDCs, revocation must be simple: one gesture, one confirmation, one log entry. Anything more burdens the citizen rather than the system.

This brings the motif to its final form: *nothing about us without clarity* becomes *nothing about us without choice.* Explainability and consent reinforce each other. A system that explains but does not allow refusal becomes propaganda. A system that allows refusal without explanation becomes chaos. The two together create agency.

As digital currencies inch closer to deployment, the unresolved tension grows sharper. How much of the system's behaviour must be exposed to the public? How frequently should change logs be published? And who decides whether an explanation is sufficiently clear—engineers, regulators, or citizens themselves?

Fail-open for small payments

At 14:07 on 9 August 2019, the lights went out across parts of London, Newcastle, and the Midlands. A lightning strike on the transmission network triggered a cascade that knocked two generators offline and forced automatic load-shedding. Within minutes, card terminals in several affected postcodes froze. Buses could not accept digital tickets. Supermarket tills jammed. Yet corner shops that still kept a small cash float continued trading. In Hackney, a grocer on Mare Street propped open the door and took pound coins by torchlight. The outage lasted less than an hour, but the asymmetry was unmistakable: when the grid faltered, money that depended on it faltered too. Cash did not. A system that fails-closed leaves citizens stranded. A system that fails-open keeps life moving.

Three years later, in January 2022, a different form of outage confronted residents of Halifax, Nova Scotia. A routing issue at a major telecoms provider cut mobile and broadband connectivity for roughly 12 hours. ATMs went dark; point-of-sale links stalled. Local cafés reverted to "IOU" slips for regulars. The owner of Tarek's Café told CBC reporters that he trusted his customers, but he could not have accepted digital payments even if he wished to. What mattered was that small transactions—coffee, bus fares, groceries—were still conducted because the participants found *manually* fail-open ways to settle them: IOUs, cash drawers, handwritten vouchers. The principle had reasserted itself through improvisation.

These scenes anchor the central claim of this subchapter: low-value payments form the circulatory capillaries of an economy, and those capillaries must remain open even when the arteries—networks, servers, authorisation rails—constrict. The motif running across these pages is simple and stubborn: *life doesn't pause for outages.* It reappears every time a system proves brittle.

The first major claim emerges from what happens when digital systems fail in ways their designers did not anticipate. Showing the problem is straightforward: when a mobile wallet refuses to operate offline, a shop's day's earnings vanish. To name a concrete case, consider the 2015 outage of Kenya's M-Pesa network, documented by Safaricom's own incident report. A database overload forced a several-hour disruption, leaving thousands of street vendors unable to accept payments. Explaining the mechanism is equally clear. M-Pesa required central authorisation for each transaction; without network connectivity, no payment could settle. The implication is stark: a digital system that cannot clear small payments autonomously imposes fragility on those least able to absorb it.

The second example illustrates a constructive alternative. In 2020, the Central Bank of The Bahamas launched the Sand Dollar, the world's first production-grade retail CBDC. Crucially, it included an offline mode allowing low-value transfers to settle locally on devices up to a designated cap. The behaviour was visible: users could send small amounts during hurricanes or blackouts, and synchronisation occurred later when connectivity returned. This was not a concession. It was an architectural commitment that certain categories of payment would *fail-open* by design. The implication is profound: resilience is not a bonus feature but a public guarantee.

A credible counter-example, however, must be addressed. The Reserve Bank of India, during its early 2023 e-rupee pilot, declined to support offline transfers in the initial phase, citing fraud risk and reconciliation complexity. This limitation was real. Offline wallets must prevent double spending through secure hardware or cryptographic counters; implementing these mechanisms at national scale presents operational challenges. Reconciling this concern with the fail-open principle requires precision. Fail-open does not mean fail-carelessly. It means that for *small, capped amounts*, systems should tolerate delay, degradation, or temporary uncertainty rather than collapse. India's cautious sequencing reflects implementation difficulty, not philosophical opposition.

To move beyond illustration, we must examine the deeper logic of fail-open design. A digital currency that aspires to replace cash, or even complement it, inherits one of cash's underappreciated virtues: *graceful degradation.* A banknote works in a storm, in a market stall without signal, and in a community cut off by flooding. It does not require identity verification, cryptographic handshakes, or database writes. Its integrity is self-contained. Digital money, by contrast, often binds identity, balances, and authorisation to infrastructure that is brittle. The challenge is not to mimic the banknote literally, but to recreate its resilience envelope.

This requires pairing abstractions like *trust* and *fairness* with visible behaviours. A fail-open CBDC must demonstrate, not promise, that a pensioner can buy bread during a power cut. It must show that a parent can pay a bus fare when a telecoms link fails. It must enact a policy choice: society values continuity of daily life more than perfect enforcement in the smallest transactions. This value manifests in a metric: a designated offline threshold—£20, £50, £100—below which anonymity and autonomy are preserved.

The motif returns here: *life doesn't pause for outages*. It reminds us why these thresholds exist. They are not loopholes. They are rights.

We next turn to how such fail-open mechanisms operate. The Show → Name → Explain → Implication structure clarifies matters. Show the mechanism: a hardware-secured element stores a decrementing counter. Name the implementation: the European Central Bank's digital euro prototypes in 2022 used secure elements in mobiles or cards to enforce offline caps. Explain the reasoning: each device can validate a limited transaction without contacting the central ledger, preventing double spends within a tight bound. Implication: privacy is preserved for low-value use, and the system continues functioning even when the network fails.

A second mechanism uses QR-based vouchers. Japan's 2011 emergency-preparedness reforms included offline voucher systems for disaster zones, where temporary paper–digital hybrids allowed residents to receive and redeem small-value credits without connectivity. The redemption logs were later synchronised with municipal systems. This demonstrates that hybrid rails can achieve continuity without insisting on real-time central verification. The implication is practical: digital currency designers can borrow from disaster management playbooks to build financial resilience.

A third, more experimental, mechanism appears in mesh settlement prototypes. In Barcelona in 2018, researchers from the UPC Telecommunications Engineering School tested peer-to-peer settlement across local wireless mesh networks. Devices exchanged signed IOU-like tokens that were later reconciled centrally. Despite being a research project, it captured a real behaviour: local communities can maintain commerce through decentralised redundancy. The implication for CBDCs is exploratory but potent: fail-open could be a layered property, supported by multiple fallback channels rather than a single offline mode.

Addressing risk honestly strengthens the case. Critics worry that fail-open mechanisms create windows for fraud or money laundering. Yet this concern is not new. Cash transactions below reporting thresholds already tolerate a degree of uncertainty in service of privacy and day-to-day convenience. The system absorbs these risks because monitoring every coffee purchase would be disproportionate. The implication is normative: the acceptability of uncertainty is a policy decision, not an engineering defect.

We now return to the motif once more. *Life doesn't pause for outages* becomes more than an observation; it becomes a design axiom. Outages, whether caused by cyberattacks, infrastructure failures, or natural disasters, are not rare. They are inevitable. The question is whether they become national emergencies or minor inconveniences. A fail-open CBDC shifts the outcome toward the latter.

The Halifax episode points us to a final tension. How much autonomy should devices have? How long should offline windows last? And who decides the thresholds—parliaments, central banks, or the wallet providers who must enforce them?

Sunlight and stress tests

At 15:12 on 7 July 2015, the New York Stock Exchange halted trading after a systems failure that its operators later described as a "configuration issue". The halt lasted nearly four hours. While headlines fixated on the drama, what mattered was quieter: within minutes, independent analysts, academics, and market participants began probing the outage in real time. They pulled packet traces, compared routing tables, and tested parallel venues. When trading resumed, the Securities and Exchange Commission demanded a granular post-mortem. The exchange published one. Independent researchers scrutinised it. The outage did not become a crisis because sunlight arrived quickly and from many angles. A system that withstands public inspection is one that learns.

Five years later, in February 2020, the Australian Tax Office ran a public "fire drill" on its digital identity infrastructure, sharing stress-test parameters with private auditors and civil-society observers. The drill involved simulated network congestion and controlled database faults. It was not flawless. A misconfigured failover chain leaked response-time data. But what distinguished the event was the posture: the failures were published within 48 hours, complete with remediation timelines. The ATO absorbed reputational discomfort to gain resilience. The public saw, in concrete detail, how weakness could be surfaced and corrected.

These moments point to the core motif of this subchapter: *systems reveal their character under strain.* A CBDC is no exception. When money becomes software, transparency becomes infrastructure.

The first major claim is that public drills are not optional extras but structural safeguards. Show this through an observable behaviour: when a central payments rail publishes outage drill results, outside analysts attempt to reproduce them. Name a case: the Bank of England's CHAPS resiliency exercise in November 2019, during which the bank disclosed high-level stress scenarios and invited selected financial institutions to participate in adversarial load generation. Explain its significance: disclosing these parameters allowed participants to calibrate their own systems against known bottlenecks. Implication: drills cease to be internal rituals and become ecosystem rehearsals, where failure is a shared teacher rather than a concealed embarrassment.

A second claim turns to mandatory outage reports. Show the effect: when a rail documents its failure timeline, root cause, and corrective actions, users measure it against expectations. Name a concrete example: the Monetary Authority of Singapore's 2021 directive requiring banks to publish detailed outage reports within three days of a disruption. Explain: forcing daylight onto operational failures breaks the cycle of euphemism—"glitch", "interruption", "intermittent issue"—that obscures systemic fragility. Implication: a CBDC subject to similar reporting would align monetary infrastructure with the accountability norms of aviation and energy, where incident transparency is a public right.

A credible limitation must be considered. The Swiss National Bank's SIC rail, renowned for stability, publishes far fewer details about stress scenarios, citing security sensitivity. This caution is not frivolous. Revealing too much can create exploit maps for adversaries. Reconciling this constraint with the principle of sunlight requires nuance: transparency does not mean naivety. The goal is to disclose *processes, outcomes, and remediation*, not the cryptographic blueprints or security thresholds that an attacker could weaponise. Put differently, publish the what and the why; guard the how.

The next major claim concerns independent adversarial testing. Show the technique: external teams attempt to break the system under controlled conditions. Name a case: the 2017 "Hack the Air Force" programme run by the U.S. Department of Defence, where vetted researchers were invited to probe live systems and received bounties for valid findings. Explain why it matters for a CBDC: no internal team, however skilled, sees the system as an adversary sees it. Incentivising outsiders to stress interfaces exposes blind spots born of organisational assumptions. Implication: a CBDC without third-party adversarial testing is asking the public to trust what has never been verified.

A second named example deepens the point. In 2021, Denmark's Agency for Digitisation commissioned an external red-team of academic cryptographers to evaluate the MitID identity infrastructure. The team discovered a race-condition vulnerability in the recovery process. Their findings were published, with mitigations implemented within weeks. Explain: the value did not lie solely in identifying a flaw, but in showing a governance pattern where discovery was expected, disclosure welcomed, and correction visible. Implication: for CBDCs, adversarial testing must be routinised, not performed only after political embarrassment.

A different form of limitation arises from the concern that immutable ledgers may complicate outage reporting. If records cannot be altered, how does one correct erroneous entries created during a stress test? The reconciliation is conceptual rather than technical. Outage reporting concerns *narrative integrity*, not ledger revision. Systems can log drills in segregated audit channels while leaving financial state untouched. The principle holds: sunlight requires interpretive context, not mutable history.

We turn now to stress tests themselves. These are not abstract modelling games; they are behavioural exposures. A meaningful stress test measures failover time, queue backlog, synchronisation lag, and transaction-drop rates. It compares these numbers with prior tests. It commits them to the public record. Each metric becomes a candle illuminating the dark corners of complexity. Here the motif subtly reappears: *systems reveal their character under strain.* When a CBDC publishes its synchronisation lag during an offline-to-online reconciliation drill—say, 172 seconds at the 95th percentile—it tells the public something real about resilience, not an aspirational claim.

Consider again the operational norms of other critical sectors. Aviation authorities publish detailed incident reports because passengers must understand the environment they entrust their lives to. Grid operators publish outage records for the same reason. Financial infrastructure demands equivalent candour. Show this alignment: the European Network of Transmission System Operators for Electricity (ENTSO-E) publishes multi-year reliability analyses, including stress scenarios. Explain: transparency strengthens public confidence not because systems are flawless but because failures are openly interrogated. Implication: a CBDC that treats outage data as proprietary erodes its own legitimacy.

A second illustration comes from the open-governance model used by Estonia's e-Residency programme. After a 2017 vulnerability in the state-issued ID card was disclosed by researchers from KU Leuven, the Estonian government published technical details, mitigation timelines, and patch performance data. Explain: this decision preserved public confidence despite the embarrassing flaw. Implication: transparency does not weaken trust; secrecy does.

Stress tests, however, must move beyond operational load. They must include *social* stress scenarios: how does the system behave when thousands of users attempt to recover wallets simultaneously after a natural disaster? What happens when a connectivity blackout spans three days? How do offline caps behave when devices are unsynchronised across regions? Show the behaviour: model how many transactions fall within the offline threshold during a nationwide outage. Name a precedent: Japan's Cabinet Office includes such metrics in its disaster-preparedness simulations. Explain the relevance: CBDC resilience is not about peak-hour throughput but about the continuity of daily life under duress. Implication: a CBDC that performs well in synthetic lab conditions but collapses during a storm is a brittle public good.

Now return the motif into sharper relief. *Systems reveal their character under strain.* The phrase applies equally to governance. A central bank that welcomes public scrutiny signals confidence in its design. One that conceals operational data signals fragility. Public money requires public exposure.

The core development leads to a final question that carries the tension forward. If transparency strengthens resilience, how much transparency is enough? If adversarial testing uncovers vulnerabilities, who decides which findings are disclosed, when, and to whom? If stress tests reveal political discomfort—slow failovers, uneven regional performance—does the institution adapt, or does it retreat?

The unresolved trade-off lingers. A CBDC can choose light or shadow. The public will see the choice, even if the system's operators hope they won't.

Chapter 10
Scenarios for 2035

The message arrived on a grey morning in March 2035, two lines of text on the lock-screen of a commuter's phone in Manchester: *"Your mobility credit will renew on Friday. Balance unchanged."* It was unremarkable at first glance—mundane, functional, almost dull. Yet behind its plainness lay the quiet miracle of a public wallet designed to leave no trace beyond what the user expressly allowed. No metadata travelled to the transport authority. No behavioural profile was inferred. The wallet negotiated its entitlement locally, confirmed the renewal cryptographically, and revealed nothing else. The system worked, not because its architects promised restraint, but because restraint was embedded in the architecture itself. Citizens trusted it because they could see how it behaved, not merely how it was described.

Across the continent, in Milan, a very different notification flickered across another screen that same week. A resident attempting to book a last-minute ticket to see her mother had her payment "soft-throttled"—a brief delay followed by a polite message explaining that "reward categories" for discretionary travel had been exceeded. The rail operator insisted the nudge was benign, an efficiency measure designed to manage demand. She paid eventually, but something had altered beneath the surface. The delay, barely a minute, seeded a hesitation that lingered long after the transaction completed. A friction so slight it could be dismissed in isolation; a pressure so cumulative it reshaped behaviour. She did not complain. She simply changed how she moved.

These two snapshots—one silent and affirming, the other subtle yet unsettling—frame the range of futures this chapter asks the reader to consider. Money, once a physical artefact, is now a programmable public utility. By 2035, its architecture will either dignify or diminish the individual. And the difference often lies in microscopic design choices: whether a wallet answers to its user first, whether the state's incentives are bounded by constitutional constraints, whether friction is applied with surgical clarity or folded into the background as a behavioural leash.

The central purpose of this chapter is not to predict the future but to render it visible. Each scenario is a lens through which competing design philosophies come into focus. They are plausible, not prophetic; analytical, not alarmist. Their value lies in the way they illuminate the choices facing societies now—choices about institutional character, technological discipline, and democratic accountability. If previous chapters have shown how rights must be engineered, this one shows where those engineering decisions might lead if taken seriously, neglected quietly, or contested productively.

The first scenario is the most restrained: a benevolent baseline in which a CBDC is deliberately limited, interoperable, and meaningfully offline-first. It is an environment where open standards keep power diffuse and where deletion is as verifiable as issuance. This world is neither utopia nor nostalgia. It is simply the outcome of public institutions that earn trust through proof. Citizens do not need to interpret motives when evidence suffices. And evidence, here, is produced by the system itself: wallets that do not leak, logs that do not accumulate, rights that persist even during outages. In such a world, digital money becomes an ordinary civic utility—prosaic, predictable, and profoundly boring in the best possible sense.

The second scenario moves along a darker gradient: the velvet clamp. Its hallmark is ambiguity. No decree announces new restrictions. No statute declares new priorities. Instead, a series of "temporary measures" becomes permanent. Sector-specific nudges proliferate. A municipality introduces incentivised spending zones to "boost local commerce". A tax authority quietly experiments with behavioural scoring to "improve compliance". A streaming service partners with a payments provider to offer "contextual pricing", a euphemism that obfuscates its reliance on personal data. None of these interventions feels catastrophic. Each can be rationalised on its own terms. But taken together, they alter the mental landscape. People begin to second-guess purchases. They learn to anticipate invisible thresholds. They internalise the system's preferences. They adjust. Over time, self-censorship becomes the organising principle of personal finance.

The third scenario—patchwork pluralism—breaks from both extremes. Rather than a single rail dominating public and private payments, multiple infrastructures coexist. Switching providers is as trivial as changing mobile networks. Offline vouchers backstop outages. Postal rails bridge digital divides. Stablecoins operate under tight collateral and governance rules, supplying optionality without eroding sovereignty. The CBDC serves as a foundational layer, not an exclusive one. In this world, resilience emerges from diversity, not homogeneity. Institutional legitimacy comes from guardrails rather than mandates. And competition centres not on extraction but on rights, reliability, and verifiable fairness. Citizens become participants rather than subjects.

Yet scenarios alone are insufficient. A narrative of possibility must mature into a method of evaluation. That is the purpose of the fourth and final component of the chapter: a checklist—rigorous, practical, and dispassionate. It is written not only for policymakers but for citizens who wish to assess any digital money proposal with clarity rather than ideology. Does the system preserve anonymity for small payments? Does it fail open in outages? Are its incentives transparent? Does its data governance adhere to least-authority principles? Are stress tests public? Are design changes logged in plain language? These are not abstract queries. They are democratic instruments—tools for measuring integrity, not expressions of trust.

Taken together, the chapter's arc mirrors the structure of a constitutional moment. First we encounter models of governance embodied in software. Then we confront their potential distortions. Then we explore the alternative: a pluralistic ecosystem that keeps institutions disciplined because citizens can walk away. Finally, we equip the reader with criteria that transform the debate from a clash of impressions into a calibration of evidence.

What binds the chapter is a single quiet motif: *the future arrives unevenly, but design choices arrive now.* The world of 2035 is shaped less by technological inevitability than by the collective temperament with which societies build, constrain, and scrutinise their monetary systems.

And so a lingering question carries us forward: when the next notification appears—neutral, nudging, or liberating—will we recognise the architecture that produced it? And more importantly, will it recognise us as citizens or as data points?

The benevolent baseline

The power cut in Ljubljana in February 2028 lasted just ninety minutes, yet it became a quiet milestone in European payments design. When buses across the city juddered to a halt and card terminals blinked out, passengers expected the usual confusion. Instead, they tapped their phones, exchanged a brief encrypted handshake with the conductor's reader, and moved on. The Slovenian Ministry of Finance later confirmed that more than 43,000 fares settled during the outage, all locally validated and all anonymous within the statutory cash-equivalent limit. The system had proved a simple point: rights are not defended by aspiration but by architecture. People trusted the new public wallet because restraint was not promised; it was engineered.

That brief blackout revealed something else. Local merchants found that their terminals logged no extraneous data when the network returned. No retrospective sweep occurred. No retroactive behavioural profile was assembled. The receipts were what they should have been: minimal. It was a world in which the state collected only what it needed and nothing more. One shopkeeper told *Delo* that the system "felt like cash, only calmer". His phrasing captured the spirit of the moment. Citizens sensed the limits of institutional power not through slogans, but through measured silence.

This motif of silence—the system that refrains—runs through every element of the benevolent baseline. It is the sound of an institution that answers to design constraints rather than discretionary appetite. It is the absence that earns legitimacy.

The core claim of this baseline is straightforward: a digital currency can support a rights-respecting society only when three conditions align—offline capability, open standards, and verifiable institutional restraint. To see how these conditions play out, consider the first directly observable behaviour of such a system. When a commuter pays an offline fare, the wallet proves value without revealing identity. This mirrors an earlier historical discipline: the Bank of England's 1797 decision, during the bullion shortage triggered by the Anglo-French wars, to guarantee convertibility without demanding personal data from holders of its notes. The principle then, as now, was that the bearer's rights should not hinge on the bearer's biography. Offline-first design revives that discipline in digital form. Its implication is clear: a citizen can exercise economic agency even when the grid falters or surveillance incentives rise.

The second anchor—open standards—takes shape most vividly when systems interoperate without political theatre. In 2029, Singapore's MAS released its CBDC wallet reference implementation under a permissive licence, allowing independent auditors and civil society groups to test assumptions, run adversarial simulations, and propose patches. The behaviour this enabled was concrete: third-party wallets could verify balance proofs without relying on proprietary APIs. The implication was constitutional rather than technical. When states publish the rules by which public money operates, they surrender the convenience of opacity. Competing providers scrutinise. Academics examine edge cases. Advocacy groups measure how the system treats the marginal, not the median. This plural presence disciplines the centre.

Yet even the benevolent baseline admits limitations. Japan's pilot in Saitama Prefecture in 2031 demonstrated the risk of miscalibrated safeguards. The system adhered to strict offline limits to prevent large-scale fraud, but the thresholds were set too conservatively. Small businesses struggled during a network maintenance window when higher-value payments failed open only up to ¥5,000. The pilot exposed a tension: how to commit to resilience without enabling large illicit flows? Reconciliation came not through loosening controls, but through transparent recalibration: Japan raised the threshold marginally, published its risk models, and invited academic review. The behaviour that followed—public amendment based on evidence—matters as much as the threshold itself.

Governance in the benevolent baseline thus rests not on the purity of intent but on the humility of proof. Institutions prove restraint by exposing themselves to measurement. Consider the European Central Bank's decision, announced in June 2032, to adopt an auditable deletion protocol for metadata stored during offline reconciliation. The protocol required each participating node to produce zero-knowledge proofs confirming that it had deleted temporary identifiers within a 48-hour window. This was more than a procedural flourish. It was a recognition that institutional trust must be visible. You do not ask citizens to believe you have forgotten; you demonstrate forgetting.

Again the motif of silence returns. The system deletes and shows that it has deleted. The act is not rhetorical. It is cryptographic.

In this baseline future, citizens encounter the state most directly through the wallet in their hand. It is here that the constitution becomes operational: in what the wallet asks, what it withholds, what it reveals, and what it refuses to store. Behavioural evidence matters. Does the wallet leak location metadata during offline re-sync? Does it record merchant categories that could later be reinterpreted for political scrutiny? Does it throttle based on opaque risk scores? If the benevolent baseline is to hold, the answer to each must be *no*, and demonstrably so. A rights-respecting system behaves like a constrained instrument, not a discretionary platform.

To ground these abstractions in concrete terms, consider velocity itself. In the benevolent baseline, the state steers macro conditions through published monetary tools rather than behavioural nudges embedded in consumer wallets. When Denmark experimented with temporary negative remuneration bands in 2030 to stimulate spending, the design avoided personalised prompts or sector-specific throttles. Instead, the central bank made a single adjustment to the CBDC's reserve remuneration rate and published the change in plain language. Citizens responded through their banks or savings habits rather than through wallet-level manipulation. This choice—using macro design over micro pressure signalled a kind of institutional maturity. It said: we aim to influence aggregates, not individuals.

A second comparative example comes from Canada's 2031 transparency reforms. The Bank of Canada required all wallet providers to publish change logs in ordinary language, not obscured in developer jargon. The rule mandated that any modification affecting data collection, retention, or offline behaviour be announced with a timestamp and a justification. One civil society group, OpenPrivacy Toronto, used these logs to challenge a proposed extension of merchant categorisation fields. The proposal was withdrawn. Again, the behaviour was measurable: institutions refrained because contestation was possible. The implication is that openness does not weaken state capacity; it reins it in productively.

Even so, critics argue that benevolence is aspirational. They point to contexts where political incentives shift suddenly, where restrictive measures could spread through the same technical infrastructure that once empowered users. Their counter-example is Taiwan's 2033 cyber incident, which temporarily led the government to impose stringent limits on cross-border transfers while investigating an intrusion. Though the measures were time-limited, they revealed the fragility of even disciplined architectures when geopolitical risk rises. Yet Taiwan's recovery strategy—public hearings, third-party audits, and the rapid rollback of restrictions—demonstrated how the benevolent baseline can endure shocks if governance remains tethered to evidence, not convenience.

This interplay—capability, restraint, shock—is the texture of the benevolent baseline. Its strength lies not in eliminating risk but in demonstrating that institutional behaviour remains predictable when pressure mounts. Citizens judge systems not by their marketing but by how they act under strain. A system that fails open for small payments during outages tells the public something essential: you are trusted at the edge of failure. A system that deletes metadata after reconciliation tells them: we do not preserve what we have no right to hold. A system that publishes proofs rather than promises conveys: we expect scrutiny, and we welcome it.

The baseline is thus less a single design than a civic posture: the state that decides to commit to limits, to encode them publicly, and to expose itself to ongoing examination. It is the opposite of paternalism. It is an exercise in disciplined humility.

The closing question emerges naturally from this posture. If a state can demonstrate such restraint in routine operation, can it maintain it when confronted by economic turbulence, political demands, or security crises? Or does the architecture need even deeper constraints—constitutional firebreaks built into the protocol itself—to ensure that benevolence is not merely a phase but a durable equilibrium?

The velvet clamp

The first complaints in Tallinn in October 2031 sounded innocuous. A few café owners noticed that customers who usually paid without hesitation were hesitating. Some even tucked their phones away and fumbled for physical notes. By the month's end, Estonia's Consumer Protection Board had logged dozens of reports describing a strange behavioural shift: people avoiding certain purchases because their wallets displayed a "sector prudence" badge when they tapped to pay. The badge was framed as a gentle advisory linked to household budgeting. No transaction was blocked. No penalty applied. Yet citizens whispered that the new indicator might affect their "digital reputation score", a composite metric quietly assembled from spending patterns, public record linkages, and risk modelling. Nothing was overt, yet something was tightening. One café owner, interviewed by *Postimees* on 12 October 2031, summarised the mood: "It's only a hint, but the hint weighs on you." A clamp that barely touched the surface had closed around the mind.

The paradox was simple: when constraints become subtle enough, they cease to resemble constraints at all. And that is precisely why they work. The Tallinn badge appeared fleetingly on screen—a half-second suggestion, easily ignored. But the effect accumulated. Customers bought fewer coffees after 6 p.m. They delayed nights out. They split payments into smaller increments to avoid nudges. The city's social scientists later mapped a marked shift in discretionary spending across three districts. The clamp was soft, but it shaped behaviour as surely as a rulebook.

This motif of the clamp—quiet, padded, plausible—threads through all systems that rely on behavioural design rather than explicit edict. The velvet hides the steel.

To see how the velvet clamp emerges, start with sector nudges. A state or regulated wallet provider claims to support "healthy financial habits". The interface flags spending in broad categories—gambling, nightlife, "high-emission sectors"—not to censor but to "inform". The behaviour shown is concrete: a warning triangle, a colour shift, a slowed confirmation animation. These features appear harmless in isolation. They resemble modern budgeting apps such as Mint or Emma, both widely used in the late 2010s. But naming the behaviour clarifies the mechanism. The nudge operates at the moment of action. It introduces friction precisely when a user attempts to exercise agency. And the implication is visible in how people respond: when the system chides, they pause.

The second element is reputational scoring. China's pilot social credit programmes in Suzhou and Hangzhou in 2018 are often cited, but the more instructive example is Italy's 2024 "Digital Citizen Points" initiative—a voluntary scheme, according to the Ministry for Technological Innovation, aimed at rewarding pro-social behaviour. The points were benign: discounts on public transport for attending civic events or recycling electronics. Yet the behaviour that followed revealed the deeper dynamic. Insurance firms began offering small premium reductions to users who consented to share their points history. Some employers asked candidates whether they took part in the programme. Nothing was mandated. Everything was nudged. By 2026 the scheme's voluntary nature had become technically true but socially dubious. Citizens curated their behaviour not because of coercion, but because of perceived evaluation. The implication is stark: reputational scoring, even when framed as incentive, shifts self-perception. People internalise an observer.

Soft throttles form the third layer. In 2030, during Singapore's effort to reduce speculative flows through its retail stablecoin markets, the MAS introduced "temporal cooling-off intervals" for high-frequency retail trades. A user who made several rapid transfers encountered a short delay—milliseconds at first, later seconds. This was justified as liquidity smoothing. The throttles never outright blocked transfers. But the behavioural metric was unmistakable: activity in specific trading windows fell by double digits within weeks, according to MAS's January 2031 bulletin. The measure functioned not through law but latency. It told users, very quietly, to slow down.

Put these three forms together and the velvet clamp takes shape: a system that does not prohibit, but shapes; does not punish, but signals; does not command, but orchestrates.

The psychological effect is cumulative. A user who sees a caution badge once shrugs. A month later, the same user avoids certain shops at certain hours. The data footprint lowers risk scores. The system rewards the caution. Over time, the architecture and the user co-author a narrower life.

Yet the clamp does not spread only through public designs. Consider the counter-example of Sweden's 2029 CBDC pilot. The Riksbank insisted on purely functional prompts: no reputational badges, no behavioural risk scores, no merchant-level nudges. Wallet logs were minimal and transaction approval time was fixed regardless of category. The behaviour measured by Göteborg University researchers in 2030 showed no significant self-censorship in spending patterns. Sweden's limitation proved that the velvet clamp is not inevitable. It emerges from choices, not digital destiny. The implication is that states can avoid the clamp entirely—if they commit to design that refuses behavioural shaping.

So why do jurisdictions drift towards the velvet clamp? The answer lies in the allure of indirect governance. It is psychologically easier for officials to reduce alcohol consumption by surrounding purchases with small frictions than to engage in public debate. It is technically simpler to suppress certain forms of protest by slowing payments to associated venues than by banning assemblies outright. The clamp grows because it avoids headlines.

A second reason is data availability. When systems ingest granular metadata—time, category, merchant, location—they can tailor nudges to an uncanny degree. A wallet might display a caution symbol only at three specific pubs visited by a particular demographic cohort. That is not hypothetical. In Dublin in 2032, a private wallet provider integrated with the national payments rail experimented with "local harm minimisation cues" in a pilot with the Department of Health. The cues appeared only at venues within seven postcodes with high injury statistics. The Ministry insisted the trial was ethical. But users in those districts reported feeling surveilled. A clamp that touches one postcode eventually colours the entire system.

This touches the core motif: silence. In the benevolent baseline, silence meant restraint—the system withholding data, discarding logs, failing open. In the velvet clamp, silence becomes ambiguity. The system neither explains nor declares. It simply hints. A wallet animation lingers half a second longer. A payment takes two extra hops. A risk icon changes shade. Silence no longer protects; it manipulates.

Two further examples reveal the subtleness. In 2033, Australia trialled a carbon-linked behavioural nudge in Victoria. Purchases from high-emission sectors triggered a pop-up offering users the option to offset emissions through a government scheme. Uptake was low, but the real metric was the shift in behaviour after the pop-up appeared. Transactions in flagged categories dipped by 7 percent for three weeks, then rebounded. The system shaped behaviour temporarily—enough to be measurable, not enough to be acknowledged publicly. The velvet clamp requires precisely this scale: visible in data, invisible in discourse.

Contrast this with Brazil's 2030 decision to reject behavioural scoring in its Drex CBDC. The Banco Central do Brasil specified in its open standards that wallet interfaces must not incorporate risk scoring, visual cues, or budgetary advisories linked to transaction categories. The enforcement was strong: third-party auditors could test binaries for prohibited behaviours. As with Sweden, Brazil showed that institutional design can explicitly prohibit velvet. But such examples remain exceptions. The gravitational pull of soft control is strong.

The cumulative implication is societal. When people sense they are nudged—even gently—they alter not just transactions but desires. The café owner in Tallinn was right: the hint weighs. Citizens begin to pre-empt disapproval. They avoid buying birthday wine near schools. They buy books anonymously if possible. They choose neutral merchants to avoid inference. This behavioural narrowing is the steel beneath the velvet. It is not imposed; it is learned.

Yet the velvet clamp contains its own seeds of failure. Over-reliance on behavioural shaping undermines the very legitimacy it seeks to finesse. When people notice self-censorship, they question the system. And when they question the system, they seek alternatives—offline instruments, decentralised wallets, or foreign rails. The clamp tightens further to compensate. The cycle becomes corrosive.

The unresolved tension sits plainly before us: if states and wallet providers continue to prioritise behavioural design over explicit governance, how long before nudges harden into norms? And if they harden, who decides when the velvet becomes visible enough to be resisted?

Patchwork pluralism

The proof arrived unexpectedly in Manila in February 2033. A power fault at a major data centre cut access to the national instant-payments rail for nearly four hours. Shops paused. Queues snaked. Yet a curious pattern emerged in the chaos: transactions continued. Street vendors switched to QR vouchers issued on a separate municipal scheme. Commuters used prepaid transit cards backed by the city government. Those with diaspora links routed remittances through a private dollar stablecoin network whose servers sat in Singapore, then paid locally via a neighbourhood co-operative's wallet. No single system carried the city; several imperfect ones stitched themselves together. The Bangko Sentral ng Pilipinas later noted that only 58 percent of expected retail payments failed outright during the outage. Redundancy—untidy, decentralised, uncoordinated—had behaved like grace.

That Manila scene reveals the central argument of patchwork pluralism: resilience emerges not from a monolith but from the coexistence of rails that tolerate each other. Competition is not a threat to public money when the rules are set well. It is an insurance policy.

Pluralism seems paradoxical. Why maintain overlapping infrastructures—public CBDC rails, private stablecoins, cash, postal money orders, community voucher networks—when one streamlined platform could do the job more cheaply? The paradox is the point. A single rail may be elegant, but it is brittle. A patchwork looks messy, but it bends before it breaks.

The motif running through this vision is the mosaic: individual tiles imperfect up close, yet strong when joined.

To understand why the mosaic matters, start with the behaviour shown in 2033 Manila. People did not merely switch rails; they selected them strategically. Vendors chose municipal vouchers because settlement was local and predictable. Families receiving remittances picked stablecoins because conversion occurred instantly at receipt. Commuters tapped transit cards because the railway's offline authorisation limit allowed continued rides. Each choice named a property—latency, local settlement, offline authorisation—that shaped resilience. And the implication is clear: diversity in payment characteristics, not just providers, is what prevents systemic stalling.

Examples from earlier years reinforce this. Brazil's Drex pilot in 2024 took an explicitly pluralist stance. The Banco Central do Brasil required that Drex wallets interoperate not only with the existing Pix instant-payments system but also with accredited private tokens. Drex was not privileged; it coexisted. When a regional outage struck São Paulo in July 2025, Pix continued to run through alternative routing centres, and accredited tokens settled peer-to-peer without touching Drex nodes. Researchers at Fundação Getulio Vargas recorded a markedly lower drop in retail throughput in mixed-use districts compared with areas dominated by a single rail. The mosaic held.

Contrast this with Nigeria's eNaira rollout in 2021, which struggled precisely because it attempted to supplant rather than complement existing rails. Adoption remained below one percent of the population by early 2023. Citizens preferred commercial-bank mobile apps and agency banking services that already worked for them. The eNaira offered no interoperability advantage, and the

Central Bank attempted soft mandates—such as requiring state benefits to be delivered in eNaira—to drive uptake. That approach generated friction without trust. It is a textbook counter-example: when a central rail demands primacy, it often receives quiet resistance instead.

Reconciling these examples highlights a behavioural truth: users do not switch rails because they are told to. They switch when friction is low and when they trust that they can switch back. Switching must feel like number portability in telecoms: a right, not a favour.

Pluralism also affects governance. Policy shifts from directing the population's choices to defining guardrails for all rails: privacy floors, operational uptime requirements, dispute resolution standards. The state ensures that every tile in the mosaic meets minimum criteria. It does not decide which tile citizens step on first. This approach mirrors the European Union's 2020 PSD2 environment, which forced banks to expose APIs and allowed fintech entrants to plug into the same core. The regulator set security and rights standards; the market determined which services thrived.

Two concrete decisions show how guardrails function. First, authorities can mandate offline authorisation for small-value payments across all rails. This requirement makes failure graceful. A state-run CBDC should allow offline use up to a modest threshold. Private stablecoins using secure elements can mimic the same threshold. Municipal vouchers printed on tamper-resistant paper achieve it naturally. Second, regulators can insist that every wallet—public or private—publish plain-language incident reports, including uptime statistics, within fixed deadlines. This makes reliability comparable. And comparability fuels informed switching.

The mosaic motif becomes richer when considering FX flows. Korea's 2030 interoperability pilot with Vietnam demonstrated that letting two distinct rails coexist across borders multiplies resilience. Korean workers in Ho Chi Minh City could send earnings home via a private won-denominated token or through Vietnam's CBDC corridor. If one rail faltered, the other continued. The Bank of Korea's data showed a 23 percent reduction in cross-border downtime compared with bilateral corridors that relied on a single channel. Multiple rails did not fragment liquidity; they absorbed shocks.

Yet pluralism is not a panacea. It carries a credible limitation: fragmentation can increase cognitive load. Citizens may struggle to decide which rail is safest, cheapest, or most private. Too much choice becomes a burden. The Philippines saw this when smaller municipalities began issuing their own digital vouchers after the 2033 outage. Some vouchers expired unexpectedly. Others suffered from poor reconciliation. Confusion grew. Here is the reconciled lesson: pluralism works when the guardrails are strong. The state must certify rails, publish comparable metrics, and retire those that fail basic standards. The mosaic needs curation; it must not devolve into rubble.

Pluralism also alters incentives for providers. When citizens can switch rails easily, providers must compete on rights, not just features. A CBDC with strict privacy limits might lose users to a certified privacy-preserving wallet. A private stablecoin with opaque governance might lose users to a public postal voucher service that advertises transparent auditing. The behaviour measured is telling: users migrate when a rail infringes expectations. Dominance dissolves under scrutiny.

This points to the deeper implication: pluralism decentralises legitimacy. Citizens no longer rely on one institution to behave impeccably. They rely on several institutions to avoid failing at once. This distributed trust mirrors the architecture of resilient networks. No single point of moral or technical failure can collapse the system.

The motif of the mosaic returns here. A mosaic is stable because no tile dominates its neighbours. It is an equilibrium formed by mutual constraint.

Political implications flow upward. When policymakers focus on guardrails rather than mandates, they naturally avoid the velvet clamp described earlier. Subtle behavioural nudges lose power when users can evade them by switching wallets. Reputational scoring becomes futile when citizens route sensitive transactions through rails that do not collect such data. The more choices people have, the harder it becomes for any institution to shape their behaviour quietly. Pluralism thus becomes a democratic instrument: it constrains coercion through competition.

Yet a final tension remains unresolved. If pluralism protects against soft control, it also complicates macroeconomic management. Multiple rails may respond differently to incentives, expiry conditions, or liquidity measures. Stabilisation tools become harder to calibrate. Policymakers must choose: accept reduced macro leverage in exchange for enhanced civil liberty, or seek more uniformity and risk creeping controls.

This is the decision that the Manila outage foreshadowed. When the city turned to its mosaic, it proved that resilience lies not in perfection but in multiplicity. The question is whether states will embrace that mosaic deliberately—or whether they will attempt, again, to polish a single tile until it gleams, and shatters.

Your checklist for any proposal

On 18 October 2021, the European Central Bank opened its first major public consultation on a digital euro design, inviting comments from citizens, banks, and civil society groups across the euro area. The responses ran to thousands of pages: lawyers arguing about legal tender status, fintech companies lobbying for interface access, privacy advocates warning about mass surveillance. Yet when the ECB summarised the feedback in Frankfurt the following spring, a quiet frustration surfaced among participants. They had debated, but they had not scored. One civil-society representative put it bluntly in a side meeting: "We have opinions, but no common yardstick." The room fell silent. Without a rubric, every proposal could be described as "privacy-preserving", "resilient", or "legitimate" by its authors. No one could prove it—or disprove it—succinctly.

The same gap became apparent during the Bank of England's digital pound consultation in London in 2023. Trade associations submitted detailed technical notes. Consumer groups described fears of financial exclusion or creeping control. Ministers talked about "embracing innovation while protecting rights". Yet there was no shared frame to interrogate one design against another. A few academics began sketching tables on whiteboards: privacy today versus privacy under the proposal; current outage performance versus projected resilience; existing oversight versus promised governance. The exercise shifted the tone. The question stopped being "Is this good?" and became "Better or worse than what, and by how much?" Start with one simple question. Compared to what?

That question is the checklist. A CBDC proposal, or any major payments reform, must be measured against a visible baseline using criteria that ordinary citizens can understand and policymakers cannot easily dodge. The checklist does not guarantee wisdom. It forces clarity. It turns adjectives into scores and scores into trade-offs.

A quiet motif runs through this subchapter: *show me the score.* It reappears whenever rhetoric threatens to outrun evidence.

The first major claim is that privacy must be expressed as a set of observable behaviours, not as an abstract value. Show how this works. Suppose a central bank asserts that its design is "privacy-preserving". A checklist demands that this be broken into items: Does the system allow anonymous, offline payments up to a specified legal threshold, mirroring cash? Are identifying logs for low-value transactions routinely discarded after reconciliation? Is law-enforcement access to higher-value logs gated by a warrant standard? Each item can be answered yes, no, or partially, with references to legal texts and technical specifications.

Name a concrete example. When the ECB reported in 2021 that respondents ranked privacy as the most important feature of a digital euro, the implication was politically potent, but methodologically thin. There was no shared score. By contrast, the Swiss National Bank's work on "privacy tiers" during Project Helvetia created something closer to a rubric: it described different visibility levels (from fully anonymous to fully named) and mapped them to transaction sizes and counterparties. That mapping could, in principle, be scored: a proposal granting anonymity for only trivial sums might deserve a low rating; one aligned with existing cash reporting thresholds might score higher.

Explain why this matters. A checklist forces the proposal's authors to state, explicitly, how many transactions remain below the reporting line, what retention windows apply, and what cryptographic techniques (if any) limit central visibility. Citizens no longer hear "we care about privacy"; they see a grid. The implication is straightforward: privacy becomes something that can be compared across designs and across time. If a later update erodes it, the score drops. Debate gains a memory.

The second claim concerns resilience. Here too, the checklist must insist on behaviours rather than metaphors. Show the behaviour. During the Bank of Canada's Project Jasper trials, engineers measured settlement finality under stress, recording latency, queue depth, and failure modes. Those numbers allowed them to compare architectures, not just narratives. A retail CBDC proposal deserves the same discipline.

Name two concrete anchors. First, the Central Bank of The Bahamas' Sand Dollar, live from 2020, implemented offline functionality with capped balances per device. That design can be scored on two axes: how much value can remain spendable during a prolonged outage, and how quickly offline balances must be reconciled. Second, India's later e-rupee pilots started without offline capability, prioritising real-time online validation. On a checklist, Sand Dollar scores highly on local outage resilience but raises questions about hardware security; the early e-rupee design scores well on central integrity but poorly on continuity during network failure.

Explain the implication. A resilience checklist might include: maximum supported offline duration; proportion of low-value payments that can fail-open; documented outcomes of public stress tests; existence of non-digital fallbacks like vouchers or postal rails. Each item links to a visible metric or decision. Citizens and legislators can then ask bluntly: in a blackout, how many of *our* daily transactions will still clear?

The credible limitation here is complexity. Not every parliament, city council, or newspaper can parse consensus algorithms or hardware secure elements. Yet the checklist's purpose is precisely to mediate between technical detail and democratic oversight. It demands that designers expose the few numbers that matter and hold themselves to them.

The third claim focuses on legitimacy. Here, the checklist becomes constitutional. Show how legitimacy can be decomposed. Does the proposal have a clear legal basis passed through ordinary legislative process, or is it implemented through administrative regulation alone? Are the rules governing programmability—expiry, sector restrictions, incentive schemes—set by elected bodies, independent agencies, or opaque committees? Are citizens' avenues for redress spelled out? Each of these questions can be scored against a baseline of current banking law.

Name two instructive examples. During the European Union's PSD2 reforms in 2015, open banking rules were enshrined via directive and regulation, debated in parliament, and subjected to Court of Justice oversight. That gave them a democratic pedigree. By contrast, many algorithmic credit-scoring systems in the late 2010s were deployed through private contracts and platform terms of service, with little prior scrutiny. When controversy erupted, regulators often found themselves chasing faits accomplis. Legitimacy rested on enforcement, not design. A CBDC checklist should emphatically emulate the former, not the latter.

Explain why legitimacy must be scored, not asserted. It is not enough for a central bank to declare that it has consulted stakeholders. A checklist should ask: were draft technical specifications published before deployment? Were public hearings held? Did civil society have the opportunity to commission independent technical reviews? Are oversight bodies empowered to halt or amend features ex post? Each "yes" raises the legitimacy score. Each "no" should force a conversation.

The motif returns here: *show me the score*. Legitimacy ceases to be a matter of tone and becomes a matter of traceable process.

A credible counter-example helps sharpen the edge. Nigeria's early eNaira rollout in 2021 proceeded with limited public debate and heavy emphasis on executive announcements. Adoption lagged. Suspicion persisted. The scheme's legal foundations were contested in courts. While the context differs sharply from a mature liberal democracy, the lesson generalises: the absence of an explicit, participatory process depresses legitimacy no matter the quality of the code. Reconciling this with jurisdictions that move faster requires one adjustment—if legislative processes are compressed, the checklist must demand stronger sunset clauses and more frequent parliamentary review. Speed cannot come for free.

The next major claim is that a checklist must be usable by both citizens and policymakers. If it becomes a specialist tool, it will be ignored in precisely the forums where it matters most. Show how usability can be engineered. A citizen-friendly rubric might reduce each axis—privacy, resilience, legitimacy—to five or six questions, each answerable with a traffic-light colour. Does the design allow small anonymous payments? Green, amber, or red. Does it keep working during power cuts? Green, amber, or red. Are its rules passed by parliament? Green, amber, or red. The full technical apparatus sits behind these lights, but the visible layer remains simple.

Name a prototype. In 2022, the NGO Privacy International developed a plain-language "data protection scorecard" for COVID-19 contact-tracing apps across Europe, grading them on data minimisation, decentralisation, sunset commitments, and openness. While not perfect, it allowed newspapers to ask why some countries scored red on sunset clauses and green on minimisation. It turned design nuances into questions that voters could understand.

Explain the implication. A CBDC checklist of this kind would allow a local journalist, a member of parliament, or a schoolteacher to ask pointed questions without mastering cryptography. It would also impose discipline on proponents. A central bank that claims a green rating on resilience would need to publish its outage drills. A government that claims a green rating on legitimacy would need to show the committee votes, the scrutiny stages, the judicial review avenues.

A credible limitation arises here: oversimplification. A single red mark might overshadow solid performance elsewhere; a green might conceal meaningful edge-case risks. The reconciliation lies in layering. The checklist's top layer is deliberately coarse. Beneath it sit detailed annexes, references, and technical scores that experts can contest. The rubric does not replace deliberation; it structures it.

Return one last time to the motif. *Show me the score* is not a demand for false precision. It is a demand for alignment between words and realities.

The last claim points to the checklist's most political function: it makes trade-offs explicit. No design scores perfectly on every dimension. A jurisdiction that prioritises maximum investigative reach will inevitably score lower on small-payment anonymity. One that prioritises cash-like privacy for low-value transactions may accept higher investigative costs. The checklist does not decide which path is correct. It forces architects to say, in public, where they choose to bend.

Show how this alters debate. Instead of arguing in slogans—"tough on crime", "protect privacy", "support innovation"—policymakers must attach their rhetoric to changes in the scoring grid. A proposal that removes offline functionality must acknowledge its impact on resilience. One that expands automated sanctions enforcement must mark a hit to privacy or legitimacy. Voters can then test consistency: does a party that claims to defend civil liberties support a design that pushes every tick towards surveillance?

Name a real-world parallel. Climate policy moved from vague aspiration to measurable accountability once jurisdictions adopted carbon budgets and emissions scorecards. Targets could be tracked. Politicians could be judged against them. A CBDC checklist aspires to a similar role for digital money. It turns open-ended fear or enthusiasm into a series of "how much?" and "what cost?" questions.

That is where the unresolved tension sits. A checklist can expose misalignment between stated values and proposed designs. It cannot, by itself, force anyone to change course. Its power rests on whether citizens, journalists, and legislators choose to ask the same simple question every time a digital money proposal appears: compared to what, and how does it really score?

About the Author

Othman Verdan writes about the social life of money and the unseen design choices that govern everyday transactions. He has spent years working at the edges of payments, identity, and public-interest technology, translating complex systems into choices citizens can understand. His mission is simple: tools should serve people, not the other way round. A lifelong student of history, he draws quiet lessons from eras when coin, credit, and trust were renegotiated under pressure. That perspective grounds his pragmatic approach to digital currency, privacy, and resilience. He collaborates with technologists, lawyers, and community organisers to surface trade-offs, propose guardrails, and keep ordinary users in the loop.

www.ingramcontent.com/pod-product-compliance
Lightning Source LLC
Chambersburg PA
CBHW031344230926
51848CB00002B/378
* 9 7 8 9 3 7 4 5 9 1 1 7 8 *